Sundays with Jesus

Reflections for the Year of Matthew

James DiGiacomo, SJ

Paulist Press
New York/Mahwah, N.J.

Cover design by Sharyn Banks
Book design by Lynn Else

Library of Congress Cataloging-in-Publication Data

DiGiacomo, James.
    Sundays with Jesus : reflections for the year of Matthew / James DiGiacomo.
      p. cm.
    ISBN-13: 978-0-8091-4482-2 (alk. paper)
    1. Bible. N.T. Matthew—Sermons. 2. Bible. N.T. Matthew—Meditations.
3. Church year meditations. 4. Common lectionary (1992) I. Title.
    BS2575.54.D53 2007
    252′.6—dc22

2007016423

Published by Paulist Press
997 Macarthur Boulevard
Mahwah, New Jersey 07430

www.paulistpress.com

Printed and bound in the
United States of America

Contents

Introduction

Be doers of the word, and not hearers only (James 1:22).

These homilies for the Sundays and the major feasts of the church year appear just as they were delivered by the author at parish liturgies. They are offered as a resource for homilists looking for ideas and suggestions. They can also be used as devotional reading by anyone, homilist or congregant, and are accompanied by questions that may stimulate personal reflection or group discussion. The content always derives from the gospel passages, together with frequent references to the other readings of the day.

The reader will notice that the homilies are not very long. This is because the author is convinced that parish communities appreciate preaching that is not only enlightening and inspiring but also brief, clear, and to the point. Most parishioners do not care for rambling repetitiveness. These homilies aim at economy of language and richness of content. Whether they succeed or not is for the hearer or reader to judge.

Preachers who take their task seriously are always aware that they stand on the shoulders of others. None of us can remember all who contributed to our insights, but in this case special acknowledgement is owed to the commentaries of William Barclay, William Gleason, John Kavanaugh, Dennis Hamm. Dianne Bergant, and John R. Donahue. They all aimed at contributing to good preaching, and it is hoped that this volume will serve as evidence of their skill.

Advent and the Christmas Season

Isa 2:1–5; Rom 13:11–14; Matt 24:37–44

It is the hour now for you to wake from sleep.

Today is the beginning of a new church year. We begin with the season of Advent, a time of expectation when we look forward to celebrating the birth of Christ. Christmas is a time when Jesus can come into our lives in a special way. How can we help make it happen?

Isaiah and the psalmist tell us to do just what we are doing now: go to the house of the Lord, so that he may instruct us in his ways and we may walk in his paths. Paul tells us to wake up: the night is far spent and the day is near. Cast off the deeds of darkness—carousing and drunkenness, lust and quarreling, and jealousy—and put on the Lord Jesus Christ. Clean up your life and make room for him. Jesus himself tells us to be watchful and alert. Don't be like people of Noah's time, who were caught unawares by the flood and swept away. The Son of Man will come when you least expect him.

These four men share a vision. They see the world as a place where God is active. It's a dangerous world, but one in which safety can be found by those who open themselves to God's grace. Christ came among us to satisfy the deepest longings of the human heart. One of those longings is for peace—peace among nations, peace in our families and neighborhoods, peace within our very selves. Some of that peace seems so far away! When Isaiah speaks of nations beating their swords into plowshares, it sounds like wishful thinking. But that is what hope is all about: the refusal to give in to despair. A wise man once observed that people who suffer from sorrow or depression are often unable to imagine a world different from the one in which they find themselves. Advent and Christmas remind us of what we need to remember in times like these: that a better world is possible, and that God has joined us in the struggle to make it happen. That is what we mean when, at Christmas time, we will hail the birth of Christ as the coming of the Prince of Peace.

Meanwhile, peace and justice begin in our own hearts and our own lives. Hatred, violence, and fear dominate the headlines, but we don't have to be overwhelmed by them. We can refuse to hate. We can refuse to support violence. We can refuse to give up hope. These days, that's a big order. But in our efforts to widen the circle of goodness, God has made a big investment. He has sent his only-begotten Son to be with us and to save us. During this Advent season, let's make ready to welcome him.

What helps us refuse to hate and hold on to hope? How can I refuse to hate?

Second Sunday of Advent

Isa 11:1–10; Rom 15:4–9; Matt 3:1–12

Prepare the way of the Lord.

John the Baptist was the most famous preacher of his day. He was a colorful figure who looked like the last man standing on the television reality show *Survivor*. His open-air chapel on the banks of the Jordan River was the "in" place to be, and it attracted all kinds of people. His message was exciting: the Messiah was coming, and it was time to get ready. His ritual was dramatic: confess your sins, walk into the river, be submerged, and come back up ready for a whole new life.

He was pretty hard on his congregation. He told them all to clean up their lives before it was too late. The most prominent and respected people, Pharisees and priests, members of the religious establishment, he called "a brood of vipers." If they passed the hat around, that must have cut down on the collection. But John wasn't out to make friends; he was telling them what the coming of Jesus Christ meant—good news if you were good, bad news if you were bad and refused to shape up. Being members of the chosen people wasn't a guarantee of salvation; you had to live up to your calling.

In a few weeks we will celebrate the coming of the Messiah, the birth of Jesus Christ. In a few minutes, we will profess our belief that he will come again in glory to judge the living and the dead. This is a side of Jesus that we are not always comfortable with. We'd much rather think of him as the one who heals and encourages and consoles. He is all of these things. But we can learn something important from the Baptist. He was not going to let his baptism just be a bit of religious formalism, an exercise in harmless piety; he was determined to reach people at the core of their being. The same goes for Advent. Preparing for Christmas involves not only celebration but also introspection. How ready are we for the coming of Christ?

Today's readings point the way. Isaiah says the Messiah will judge the poor with justice. The psalmist sings that justice will flourish in his time, and fullness of peace forever. Paul prays that God will enable us to live in perfect harmony with one

3

another. Peace and justice—that is what Jesus is about. John the Baptist tells us to reform our lives and to give some evidence that we mean it. As we make ready for Christmas, let us resolve to live justly, and thus make ready to welcome the Prince of Peace.

Recall a time when some religious activity reached you at a particularly deep level of experience.

Third Sunday of Advent

Isa 35:1–6a, 10; Jas 5:7–10; Matt 11:2–11

Go and tell John what you hear and see.

John the Baptist lived most of his life outdoors. When he found himself imprisoned in a cell, he must have felt trapped, with no hope of finding a way out. He must have wondered if his life's work had come to nothing. Maybe he was running out of patience; maybe he felt hope beginning to fade. So he sends messengers to ask Jesus, "Are you the one who is to come, or should we look for another?" Jesus sends back word: Don't ask who I am, look at what I have done. The blind see, cripples walk, the deaf hear, the dead rise, and the poor have the good news preached to them.

Since 9/11, we have all been in a kind of prison. We live in fear, wondering when and where the next attack will come. We hear about and experience destruction and loss of life, we face an uncertain future, and there is no end in sight. Our patience is worn thin, we get on one another's nerves, and hoping for better things looks like wishful thinking. At this depressing moment in our history, what does God say to us in today's readings? Isaiah says to those who are frightened: "Be strong, fear not! Here is your God, he comes with vindication." James says we must be patient and steady our hearts, because the coming of the Lord is at hand.

This coming of the Lord is what we are looking forward to in Advent. When the child born in Bethlehem came to manhood, he cured the blind and the deaf and the sick and raised the dead to life. We call those great deeds miracles, but they were meant as signs pointing to what was to come. In his body, which is the church, he still confronts every kind of human weakness. There are all kinds of blindness all around and within us, kinds that eyeglasses can't help; the church helps people to see what's important, what life is really all about. The gospel is preached in season and out of season, even to those too deaf to hear. Christ in his church reaches out to the poor, the lonely, the discouraged, the sick, and the dying. In baptism we are raised to new life, in the Eucharist we hear the good news and eat the bread of life. From day to day, we and our neighbors are challenged to rise above selfishness and anger and every kind of self-deception and make the world around us a better place. In a time of uncertainty and fear, we are consoled by the assurance that God cares and watches over us. And when the end of life approaches, the sacraments of the sick and the dying accompany us on our final journey.

When Jesus' message came back to John, it gave him hope and courage to face whatever might come. The same message comes to us today, as we prepare to celebrate the coming of Christ at Christmas. Then we will be able to say once again, with Isaiah, we "see the glory of the LORD, / the splendor of our God."

How can the gospel message help me to deal with our national experience of uncertainty and fear?

Isa 7:10–14; Rom 1:1–7; Matt 1:18–24

You are to name him Jesus.

"What shall we name the baby?" Different cultures at different times have various customs and ways of naming children. In some European countries, they are named after their grandparents. In this country, parents often name their children after themselves or even after movie stars. We Catholics usually choose the name of a saint. In ancient times, the newborn's name often reflected the hopes that the parents had for their child. That was how Jesus got his name.

The angel tells Joseph that he and Mary are to call the child *Jesus,* meaning "Yahweh saves," because he is destined to save his people. To the Jews of his time, this meant being saved from the Roman army that occupied their country. But Jesus was not to be a messiah who would win a military victory over their enemies; he was to save them—and us—from our *sins*.

What does that mean? Well, think for a moment what the words *saving* and *safety* bring to people's minds today. We want to keep our nation safe. We have stockpiles of nuclear and conventional weapons as insurance against enemy attacks. We have a Department of Homeland Security taking elaborate precautions to protect us from terrorists. All these measures are designed to save us from enemies *outside* who want to harm and destroy us. But not all our enemies are outside us. Some are within, and they are what we call *sins*. It is from these that Jesus comes to save us.

What are sins, anyway? Not just the breaking of rules. They are the acting out of our worst instincts: greed, anger, lust, selfishness, cruelty, envy. We all know that we have these enemies within us; when we let them out, they do harm to others and to ourselves. They keep us from reaching out to those who love us or need us. Sometimes they take the forms of apathy or self-absorption that don't make us do wrong but prevent us from doing good. And then there are the sins of weakness that lead to aimlessness, irresponsibility, and addiction.

In a few days we are going to celebrate the birth of our Lord and Savior, Jesus Christ. It's a joyful feast for many reasons. There are family reunions, the exchanging of gifts, and countless acts of generosity to those in need. Christmas brings out the best in people, and this is not surprising because that's why Jesus came—to bring out the best in all of us.

What are the enemies within me, and how can I deal with them?

Christmas

Isa 9:1–6; Titus 2:11–14; Luke 2:1–14

*She wrapped him in swaddling clothes
and laid him in a manger.*

One Christmas night, during the First World War, a strange, remarkable thing took place in the trenches. For several hours the two sides informally agreed on a truce. The shelling and the firing came to a halt, and all was silent. Then the soldiers on one side sang a Christmas carol. As the last notes faded on the night air, the soldiers on the other side sang a hymn of their own. During the next few hours the singing went on, back and forth, across No Man's Land. It was a sad and poignant scene, but it was inspiring, too. For a little while men refused to be dehumanized, enemies remembered their common humanity, and they briefly became brothers again. Such is the power of Christmas.

Some would say that, on that memorable Christmas night, the soldiers were trying to escape from reality. In a way, those few moments of peace and harmony must have seemed unreal. But were they? Look at the classic paintings of the Holy Family that appear on religious Christmas cards. Everything and everyone looks so colorful, neat, and peaceful. But, in reality, the birth took place in dirty, smelly, drafty surroundings, the last kind of place you would choose to bring a child into the world. So are the Christmas card pictures unrealistic? In a way, yes. But in another, more important, way, the paintings have it right. They see beyond the grimy trappings to a deeper reality, the coming into the world of God's own Son, the Prince of Peace. Mary and Joseph felt more than the pain and the cold; they rejoiced in the birth of a child.

Today, in the midst of wars, genocide, famine, terrorist threats, and every other kind of bad news, we celebrate Christmas because we see more deeply. We see not an abandoned world plumbing the depths of violence and hate, but a world loved by God, visited and saved by him. Like those soldiers in World War One, we see beyond the wreckage and the pain and we sing happy hymns. We look across the battle lines and see not enemies but our brothers and sisters. We celebrate a deep-down joy that refuses to be extinguished because it comes from God himself. Merry Christmas!

What can I do to make the spirit of Christmas endure in the face of conflict?

Holy Family

Sir 3:2–7, 12–14; Col 3:12–21; Matt 2:13–15, 19–23

Take care of your father when he is old.

When we think of family, the image most of us get is that of parents and growing children. So it is with our picture of Jesus,

Mary, and Joseph. But in today's first reading, Sirach reminds us of another form that families take when parents are growing old and their children have reached their middle years. This is when roles are often reversed, when caregivers now become dependent and grown children find themselves taking on burdens they thought were over when their own children left the nest. Thanks to the great progress of modern medicine, more and more people live longer than they once did. In many ways this is a great blessing, but it also brings challenges that previous generations did not have to face in such great numbers and for so long.

In Sirach's time, old age came much sooner and usually didn't last as long. For that matter, we only have to go back a couple of generations to realize how different it used to be. In the early 1950s there was a play and a movie called *Marty* that was very realistic and won several awards. In one scene, Marty's Aunt Mary, a widow, moves in with him and his mother. She had lived with her son's family but couldn't get along with her daughter-in-law. In a revealing conversation with her sister, she complains about feeling useless and on the shelf. "My life is over," she says. She was only fifty-six! That's how much times have changed.

Sirach says, "My son, take care of your father when he is old....Even if his mind fail, be considerate with him." There are many limitations that come with old age, but not all at once. Some are debilitating, others are just annoying; some are amusing, some try the patience of those concerned. You've had, or seen, or heard them all—the "senior moments," the endless conversations about ailments and treatments, the tendency to live in the past, the growing and sometimes total helplessness. But that's not the whole story. Age often brings with it real strengths. The elderly are usually wiser, thanks to their experience and the larger perspective they bring to problems and conflicts. They have had more time to learn tolerance and master patience. They can indeed be a burden, but they can also enrich the lives of their children and grandchildren in marvelous ways.

Every family's story is different. But the older we get, the more we appreciate what our parents did for us. Now we get a chance to pay them back. And here's a word of advice: Don't wait too long. When they're gone, there will be things you wish you had done for them and with them. Some of your fondest recollections will be of the times you went out of your way to return their love. For now, let's try to make the best of the so-called golden years.

How am I handling the golden years—my own, or those of others? Who are the ones I admire for the way they are handling the challenges of aging?

Solemnity of Mary, Mother of God

Num 6:22–27; Gal 4:4–7; Luke 2:16–21

Mary kept all these things, reflecting on them in her heart.

Every mother wonders about her newborn baby: how will this child turn out? What kind of life will my son or daughter have? What lies in store for this little bundle of possibilities? Even while she works around the clock to care for the infant, she has thoughtful reveries, imagining their future together as the child goes through infancy, childhood, adolescence, and adulthood. So much is possible, so much is uncertain, so much is waiting to happen.

Every child is special, but Mary knew her child was special in a way granted to no other. How the drama would play out she did not know. When she tried to put her wonder into

10

words, she exclaimed to Elizabeth, "The Mighty One has done great things for me!" (Luke 1:49). And so she reflected and pondered and meditated and turned the mystery over and over, not only in her mind but also, and more important, in her heart. For the mind can hardly grasp, but the heart can open itself to the miracle of the Word made flesh.

All her life, Mary went through what every mother goes through in bringing up a child. She experienced joy, pain, anxiety, hope, puzzlement, satisfaction, frustration, fear, surprise, disappointment, and pride. Maybe she gradually came to realize what we know, that in becoming the mother of God she has become the mother of all of us. Every mother wants to give her child so much; this mother gave us God himself. No wonder we say to her, "Hail, full of grace, the Lord is with you! Blessed are you among women, and blessed is the fruit of your womb, Jesus, the Son of God himself."

What are some of the things about my life that would make Mary proud of me?

Epiphany

Isa 60:1–6; Eph 3:2–3a, 5–6; Matt 2:1–12

Raise your eyes and look about; / they all gather and come to you.

We're all familiar with the expression "different strokes for different folks." It's a way we have of getting along with others. The world would be a much less interesting place if we were all the same. So, as long as nothing very big is at stake, we try to be tolerant and accepting of the differences in one another. The more we do this with regard to differences in race, nationality, and culture, the better the chance we have to live in peace and harmony. It's what makes us different from the racists and bigots.

Today's feast is about dealing with differences in religion. Matthew tells the story of the magi to make it clear that Christianity is for everyone. Some of the first Christians, who were Jewish, were wondering if there was a place in the church for Gentiles. The magi come from far off in the East, and they represent the wider, non-Jewish world that is waiting to hear the gospel. Since Jesus Christ came into the world, his followers have journeyed all over the world to tell people that God loves everyone, that we are all his sons and daughters, and that none of the differences among us is that important. It is a message that has the power to overcome all the things that make us enemies. When the gospel is preached in its purity and lived with integrity, there is no place for racism, sexism, ageism, or any other *ism* that corrupts and divides. At its best, Christianity has been a unifying force, helping people of nations and cultures all over the world to practice justice and live in peace.

That's Christianity at its best. But Christianity isn't just an idea; it's people. And we Christians have not always been at our best. From time to time, down through the centuries, we have fallen into the horrifying kind of behavior that now bedevils the Middle East, where religious differences turn people into violent enemies. But we have learned, and continue to learn, from our mistakes.

This feast of the Epiphany reminds us not only to tolerate but also to respect people of other faiths. Religious pluralism is a fact, and the world needs people not to be the same, but to accept one another and our differences. Different strokes for different folks. To the Jewish people of Jesus' time, the magi looked pretty exotic. "How's that? You were sent here by a *star*? That's not the way we do it!" But the magi bear witness that God calls people in many different ways. In this Christmas season, as we thank God for coming among us as a child, let's rejoice in those who, like the magi, have come from far away.

How can we take religion seriously without letting it divide us?

Baptism of Our Lord

Isa 42:1–4, 6–7; Acts 10:34–38; Matt 3:13–17

He shall bring forth justice to the nations.

When we watch Jesus being baptized by John, we are given new insight into his person and his mission. We also get a pre-figurement of our own baptism and our role in the drama of salvation that began at the river Jordan.

The Jewish people who asked John to baptize them were doing something very unusual. Baptism was a ritual reserved for Gentiles who wished to be received into the Jewish faith; Jews did not see it as a need for themselves. It was a penitential rite for people who had been shut out by God and wished to be accepted by him; the chosen people could not think of themselves that way. So the popular religious movement going on at the river was a sign that they recognized their need for God in a new way. This was the moment Jesus had been waiting for. In being baptized, he would identify himself with the people who were renouncing sin and searching for God, and he would set out on his mission to save them.

This was how his public life began. The Spirit of God descended upon him, and a voice from heaven declared, "This is my beloved Son." It recalls the words of the prophet Isaiah, "Here is my servant whom I uphold, / my chosen one with whom I am pleased." In the reading from the Acts of the Apostles, Peter said that it all began "after the baptism that

John preached,...God anointed Jesus of Nazareth with the Holy Spirit and power."

And how was he going to save them? Peter says, "He went about doing good and healing all those oppressed by the devil." Thus he fulfilled the prophecy of Isaiah: "I, the LORD, have called you for the victory of justice / ...to open the eyes of the blind, / to bring out prisoners from confinement, / and from the dungeon, those who live in darkness."

What Jesus received from John at the river Jordan was not the sacrament of Christian initiation, but it does prefigure our baptism. When you and I were baptized, not only were we adopted into the very life of God, but in our own way we too were called to go about doing good, to stand up for justice, to open the eyes of the blind, and to free people from all kinds of prisons. When we try to live up to our mission, the Lord says of us, "Here is my servant whom I uphold, / my chosen one with whom I am pleased."

How am I called to open the eyes of the blind and work for justice?

Lent and Holy Week

Ash Wednesday

Joel 2:12–18; 2 Cor 5:20—6:2; Matt 6:1–6, 16–18

Return to me with your whole heart.

There are many different ways of approaching the holy season of Lent. Some like to give up things, in a spirit of penance. Others like to put a more positive spin on it, looking for ways to become a better person. The prophet Joel puts it this way: Come back! Return to the Lord your God.

We can all look back on times when, in some ways at least, we were better than we are now. Maybe I used to be more patient. Maybe I used to be less wrapped up in myself, and more attentive toward those around me. Maybe I used to do my job with more energy and care. Maybe I used to be more generous. Whatever it is, it's a version of myself I'd like to get back to. Getting back may involve giving something up, or just adding something new to the mix that is myself. Well, here comes Lent, a time of opportunity. St. Paul tells us, "Now is a very acceptable time; behold, now is the day of salvation."

What good habits would I like to return to?

Gen 2:7–9; 3:1–7; Rom 5:12–19; Matt 4:1–11

*The Lord, your God, shall you worship,
and him alone shall you serve.*

We are all familiar with the expression "to be in denial." It means hiding from some truth about ourselves. We all do it sometimes. In the case of people with addictions—to alcohol or drugs or gambling—the need to admit the truth is crucial; otherwise they cannot be helped. That's why, in twelve-step programs, new members introduce themselves to the group by saying, "I'm so-and-so, and I'm an alcoholic (or an addict or a compulsive gambler)." That's when they stop living the lie and start to face the truth.

The Creation story is about two people in denial. Adam and Eve are creatures, dependent on God for their very being. But the serpent, the father of lies, tempts them with an illusion of self-sufficiency: "Eat of the tree and your eyes will be opened and you will be like gods." This is not a piece of ancient history but a description of the human condition, and it is very up-to-date. Like the serpent, some people today present God as one who is jealous of our happiness. They tell us to be free—and to choose without guilt. Right and wrong are whatever we decide. We are accountable to no one but ourselves. "You will be like gods who know what is good and what is evil." "If you think it's right, it's right for you." "Don't impose your morality on others." These messages come to us mainly from mass media and entertainment. You should experience whatever you desire, and relate intimately with whomever you wish...and don't let anyone tell you that you shouldn't! It's your choice!

So Adam and Eve eat of the tree, and their eyes are opened. They are naked and ashamed, no longer at peace with themselves or each other. They are just like much of our society today, conflicted and confused.

This temptation—to be completely self-sufficient, needing no one's wisdom or guidance—is rejected by Jesus in today's gospel reading. Three times the devil tempts him to go it alone, to do it all by himself. Jesus answers him: "The Lord, your God, shall you worship / and him alone shall you serve." He reminds us that no one is an island; that we are accountable to one another and to God. God wants what is best for us and is ready to help us, if we stop being in denial and admit our need.

Lent has just begun. It is time for us to take an honest look at ourselves, to admit our limitations, and to reach out to God for help. With the psalmist, we pray:

Be merciful, O Lord, for we have sinned.
I acknowledge my offense,
    and my sin is before me always....
A clean heart create for me, O God,
    and a steadfast spirit renew within me.

Look back on a time when you were in denial about something important. Where do you see the Adam and Eve story being acted out in your life?

Second Sunday of Lent

Gen 12:1–4a; 2 Tim 1:8b–10; Matt 17:1–9

Go forth...to a land that I will show you.

We're listening to a conversation between Abraham and Sarah:

Abraham: Sarah, we're picking up stakes and leaving this country. Get Lot to help you pack.

Sarah: You can't be serious! What's the problem? We're doing fine here, and moving is a big step. We're not getting any younger, you know.

A: Sorry, dear, my mind is made up. This is what God wants us to do.

S: Okay, Abe, you're the patriarch. But where are we going?

A: I don't know.

S: What do you mean, you don't know?

A: God says he'll let us know when we get there.

S: Abe, you've been out in the sun too long.

Now fast-forward about 1,900 years, and we're on the Mount of Transfiguration. Jesus has just been transformed and has given Peter, James, and John a glimpse of his glory, a hint of his divinity. Peter is so carried away that he doesn't want the moment to end, he never wants to leave this holy place. But the vision doesn't last; they are all brought back to earth. And now Peter remembers a conversation he had with Jesus just a few days ago, right after Jesus called him a rock on which he would build his church:

Jesus: All right, men, let's get moving. We're going to Jerusalem.

Peter: Are you serious? The last time we were there, they tried to kill you.

J: Yes, I know. Maybe it's time to let them have their way.

P: Nothing doing! I won't let this happen to you!

J: Get out of my way, Peter. This is something I have to do.

Sarah and Peter both made a lot of sense. They saw uncertainty and danger ahead, and wanted to stay where life was safe and predictable. Fortunately, they didn't get their way. Abraham heeded God's call, set out on his journey, and eventually became the father of a great nation, the chosen people. Jesus went to Jerusalem, suffered and died for our sins, and rose for our salvation.

Sometimes it happens this way for us, too. There are times in our lives when we think we have it made, that we've made enough sacrifices, that no one should expect any more of us, that it's time to rest on our laurels. And then, through the people around us and close to us, God calls us to leave safety and security behind and set out on new, untrodden paths to destinations unknown. Like Peter, we'd rather build a tent and settle down, but Jesus says it's time to move on. To give Peter and us courage, Jesus is briefly transformed on the holy mount; he offers a preview of the glory that awaits him and us. If we keep our eyes on him, we can follow the advice of Paul to Timothy: "Bear your share of hardship for the gospel with the strength that comes from God."

How may God be nudging me in a new or different direction?

Third Sunday of Lent

Exod 17:3–7; Rom 5:1–2, 5–8; John 4:5–42

Whoever drinks the water I shall give will never thirst.

This is a true story about three thirsty people: Jesus, the Samaritan woman, and each one of us. It was high noon in a remote, dry place where the only water came from a deep well, and Jesus didn't have a bucket. When he asked the woman for a drink, he shocked her because in addressing her he was

19

breaking some strict social taboos of that time. But when she got over her surprise, he reminded her that he was not the only one who was thirsty; so was she. He spoke of a different kind of thirst, one that could not be satisfied by water from the well. It was a thirst that we all have—a thirst for meaning, a thirst for fulfillment, a thirst for happiness that only God can satisfy.

Lent is a time when we pay more attention to this deeper thirst that is within us all. In our ordinary, day-to-day lives, we try to relieve it in a thousand ways that offer some relief but ultimately fall short. Jesus says that if we drink the water he offers, we will not be thirsty again. When do we drink this water? When we worship God in Spirit and in truth. God comes to us here in Word and Sacrament; we hear the Word of God and we eat the bread of life. This is living water, a spring welling up to eternal life.

But there is one thing more. When the Samaritan woman asks Jesus for this water, he tells her to call her husband. She says, "I have no husband." Jesus tells her that she's right. She has no husband. She's had five husbands, and the one she has now is not her husband. If she is to worship in truth, she must first get her life in order. And so must we. Lent is a time to look more closely at ourselves, to ask who we really are and what we really stand for. Are our lives in harmony with what we profess? Is there something missing? Is there something that doesn't belong?

Self-knowledge and knowing God go together. When the Samaritan woman went back to town, she told her neighbors, "Come see a man who told me everything I have done." During this holy season we should ask God to reveal us to ourselves. We may not like some of the things we see. Neither did the woman, but she got past that. Jesus didn't just scold her. He told it like it was, but he gave her the feeling that she could be different, because he believed in her more than she believed in herself. That's probably the way he feels about us.

Look back on a time when God revealed you to yourself. What is the thirst you feel the most?

Fourth Sunday of Lent

1 Sam 16:1b, 6–7, 10–13a; Eph 5:8–14; John 9:1–41

If you were blind, you would have no sin.

This is a marvelous and frightening story about people who were blind. One who was born blind came to see; that was marvelous. Others, who thought they could see, not only *were* blind, they *chose* to be blind; that is *frightening*. The enemies of Jesus closed their eyes to the truth that was right in front of them. They were living proof of the saying, "There are none so blind as those who will not see."

This story tells us something about religion, too. We know that religion can be enriching and can bring out the best in us. We must face the fact that it can also be destructive. The Pharisees took the Jewish faith, a privileged revelation from God himself, and reduced it to a series of rigid rules and regulations that almost choked the life out of it. It made them not only judgmental but also incredibly narrow. They are incapable of the most basic, natural human instincts: they are unable to rejoice in a wonderful bit of news—a neighbor who was born blind has been cured! All they can see is that one of their rules has been broken: their interpretation of the Sabbath rest has been violated. They are blind to everything else. In their moral blindness they lash out at Jesus, they bully and intimidate the parents, and they punish the man who can now see by expelling him from the synagogue.

The bad guys in this story have had a lot of company down the ages, even to our own day. The Romans persecuted the early Christians for not worshipping pagan gods. During the Crusades, Christians murdered non-Christians in the name of Christ. The trademark of racists and bigots has been a burning cross. Many of us are old enough to remember when some of our parish churches were segregated. And at this very moment fanatics who worship the same God as we, are using a corrupt version of Islam to terrorize us. War is always terrible, but worst of all are the so-called holy wars.

Religion is a powerful force, for good or for evil. It is our duty, as Christians, to keep religion pure and undefiled by narrowness, bigotry, hostility, or any other kind of blindness. That is what it means to follow Christ, the light of the world.

Look back on a time when you were blind. What made you that way?

Fifth Sunday of Lent

Ezek 37:12–14; Rom 8:8–11; John 11:1–45

I am the resurrection and the life.

Lazarus is one of three persons we read about in the gospels that Jesus raised from death to life. Of all the signs and wonders that Jesus performed, this was the most astounding. And yet the greatest of all was still to come. Lazarus was restored to life, but only for a time. Eventually he got old and sick and died. So what Jesus did at Bethany was, in the last analysis, only a reprieve from the final sentence that awaits us all. And if that were the end of the story, we would have to say that death always has the last word.

But that's not the end of the story. Two weeks from today, on

Easter Sunday, we will celebrate the final victory over sin and death. Jesus did not return to life the way Lazarus did. He rose to the fullness of life, never again to die. The raising of Lazarus was a sign, a preview of greater things to come, of wonders beyond our imagining.

We who believe in Jesus Christ know that death does not have the last word. He himself assures us in his own words: "I am the resurrection and the life; whoever believes in me, even if he dies, will live, and everyone who lives and believes in me will never die." These are the words that console us at the funerals of our loved ones. They enable us to pray, during the final liturgy, "Lord, for your faithful people life is changed, not ended. The sadness of death gives way to the bright promise of immortality." Martha and Mary got an inkling of this when Lazarus came back to them for a time. We look forward, in faith, to the ultimate fulfillment.

How does your faith help you to deal with grief and bereavement?

Palm Sunday of the Lord's Passion

Matt 21:1–11; Isa 50:4–7; Phil 2:6–11;
Matt 26:14—27:66 or 27:11–54

*Your king comes to you, / meek and
riding on...a beast of burden.*

Why did Jesus choose to ride into Jerusalem on a donkey? He was making a point.

The people waving palms were part of a triumphal procession. They were greeting a man they considered the Messiah, who they hoped would deliver them from the forces who oppressed them. For such a demonstration, a majestic horse would seem more appropriate. But Jesus was not the kind of

Messiah they expected. Matthew remembers the words of the prophet Zechariah: "Say to daughter Zion, / 'Behold, your king comes to you, / meek and riding on an ass, / and on a colt, the foal of a beast of burden.'" Not a king on a horse going out to do battle, but one who would rule in peace instead of war.

On Palm Sunday the people were greeting a king, but not the kind they expected. He will rule not from a throne but from a cross. He is indeed coming with power, but the kind of power that will not be evident for another week. Only on Easter Sunday will we understand what the parade was really all about.

Where, in my life or in the lives of those around me, is power cloaked in weakness?

Holy Thursday

Exod 12:1–8, 11–14; 1 Cor 11:23–26; John 13:1–15

This cup is the new covenant in my blood.

Holy Week is all about remembering. It's making sure that we don't forget. Forget what?

At this time of year our Jewish brothers and sisters are celebrating Passover, fulfilling God's command not to forget how they were rescued by him and given a special mission. When the family eats the lamb and the unleavened bread and bitter herbs, they recall how they were saved from death and brought out of slavery by the blood of a lamb. This is not just an exercise in nostalgia, looking back on exciting events that took place long ago. It is "a memorial feast,… which all…generations shall celebrate…as a perpetual institution." It is their way of remembering who they are.

When Jesus celebrated the Passover that final time with his band of brothers, he told them, "This bread is my body that is for you. This cup is the new covenant in my blood. Do this in remembrance of me. Don't forget." Every time we celebrate the Eucharist, we reenact the sacred drama of that first Holy Thursday. We remind one another that this is the Lamb of God who takes away the sins of the world. We don't just recall an event that happened to other people long ago and far away. Paul tells us, "As often as you eat this bread and drink the cup, you proclaim the death of the Lord until he comes." We are making present on this altar, here and now, the saving power of his death and resurrection, and we are remembering who we are—a holy people, a royal priesthood, bought with the blood of the Lamb and fed with the Bread of Life.

How do I find my identity in the events of Holy Week?

Good Friday

Isa 52:13—53:12; Heb 4:14–16; 5:7–9; John 18:1—19:42

I find no guilt in him.

In the final scene of the Academy Award-winning film *Judgment at Nuremberg*, an American judge played by Spencer Tracy confronts a convicted Nazi war criminal played by Burt Lancaster. As a civil judge, Lancaster had caved in to pressure by Hitler, convicted innocent defendants, and sent them to concentration camps. After the trial and his conviction, he asks Tracy to visit him in his cell. He admits his guilt and accepts the justice of his sentence, but he wants Tracy not to judge him too harshly in his mind. He says, "I want you to know... you must understand...I never thought it would come to this [the concentration camps]." Tracy looks at him for a long moment, and the audience expects to hear a word of understanding, a realization that Lancaster had not foreseen the horror of the camps. Instead, he says, "It came to this, the first time you condemned an innocent man."

Pontius Pilate never thought it would come to crucifixion. After hearing the charges and examining the prisoner, he tells his accusers: "I find no guilt in him." And that should have been the end of it. His next move should have been to let him go. But politics and public relations with the Temple authorities made it advisable for him to compromise. If he just let Jesus go free, important people would lose face. So he tries to come up with something for everybody. He offers a choice between Jesus and Barabbas, and that doesn't work. He tries to get Jesus to let him off the hook, but gets no help from him. He even tries networking with Herod, and that gets nowhere. So he makes one last attempt. He'll have Jesus scourged, hoping that alone will satisfy the mob.

Punish him for what? For being innocent? For being falsely accused? For getting caught in the middle of a power struggle between corrupt and powerful men? Pilate thought he could have it both ways, but, of course, justice and compromise never go together. He wants the impossible: to dispense justice, but not too much. He wants to be fair, but not too fair. He wants to tell the truth, but not at the expense of important people's feelings. And then the priests play their trump card: "If you release him, you are not a Friend of Caesar."

That does it. When the chips are down, you have to use your head. If Caesar, back in Rome, gets a bad report on him, think what it would mean. No more governor's palace with free limousine service and a padded expense account. No more swimming pool. Goodbye stereo system and dancing girls. Okay, guys, you win. Take him away. Just give me some water, so I can wash his blood off my hands. Don't blame me. It's his own fault. A man has to protect his own. I mean, survival is what it's all about, right? I didn't want to hurt anybody, I just wanted to do right by my family. A lot of people depend on me, and I owe them something. But I never thought it would come to this.

Sound familiar? You bet. The world hasn't changed much in two thousand years. Jesus Christ, in the person of the poor and the powerless, still suffers at the hands of the rich and the powerful. It was a dangerous environment for God to come down and be a part of, and it still is. But he loved us so much that he came, anyway. And he would do it again.

How can I make my world a safer place for those who come in the place of Christ?

Easter Season and Two Solemnities

Acts 10:34a, 37–43; Col 3:1–4; Matt 28:1–10

Do not be afraid!…He has been raised just as he said.

There's an old saying that it's never so dark as just before the dawn. That certainly was true for the followers of Jesus very early that first Easter Sunday morning. A week ago they had accompanied him on a triumphal march into Jerusalem before the celebration of Passover, the feast of national liberation. The crowd was shouting and waving branches and gave them the feeling that they were part of a popular movement that would sweep all before it. Now their hopes and dreams lay in ruins, and they had lost the will to put their lives together again,

It is in this dark, gloomy moment that the light bursts upon them. The angel tells them, "Do not be afraid! I know that you are seeking Jesus the crucified. He is not here, for he has been raised just as he said." They don't know whether to be fearful or overjoyed, so Jesus himself appears and tells them, "Do not be afraid."

To recognize the risen Jesus is to catch a glimpse of the person I am meant to be. When Christ conquered death, he did it for us all. He offers us the gift of eternal life; what will it be like? We don't know, but we have been given a sign—the resurrected body of Jesus. His risen body is *real,* but it has been

29

changed. It's really Jesus, but he's different. His body is radically transformed. He can eat, but he needs no food. He can be touched, yet he is free of the limitations of time and space. He is radiant in triumph, forever more a stranger to weariness and loneliness and pain. In suffering and laying down his life, he has banished sorrow and defeated death.

This is the message of the empty tomb: like Jesus, we will suffer and die, but we will not be destroyed. We will be changed, remarkably changed for the better. All our heart wishes will be fulfilled, beyond our wildest dreams. When Christ triumphed in the resurrection, he defeated everything that is painful, confusing, difficult, and lonely. By his total victory over sin and death, he gained everything that the human heart can wish for. By ourselves, we could never do it. But together with the risen Christ, we can. For, as St. Paul tells us, "Your life is hidden with Christ in God. When Christ your life appears, then you too will appear with him in glory."

What are the things I wish for that only Christ can give?

Second Sunday of Easter

Acts 2:42–47; 1 Pet 1:3–9; John 20:19–31

Do not be unbelieving, but believe.

We call him "Doubting Thomas," but there was a lot more to him than that. We know quite a bit about Thomas the Apostle, and the more closely we observe him, the more we learn not only about him but also about ourselves and our life of faith.

There is an incident related about him that is not as well known. When Jesus told his friends that he was going to Jerusalem for the Passover, they warned him not to go: there were powerful men there who wanted to do him harm. When

Jesus insisted, Thomas broke into the conversation. He told everyone to stop arguing and to just go with Jesus to Jerusalem and die with him. Some have called him a pessimist, but let's face it: he was a realist. And he was right. When Jesus got killed, Thomas was not surprised; it's what he expected. But even though he foresaw what might happen, he never hesitated to follow Jesus, because he loved him enough to risk his life for him.

When the resurrected Jesus appeared to his friends that first Easter Sunday, Thomas was not with them. Like the others, he had cancelled all his dreams and expectations. Unlike the others, he decided to face his broken heart alone, by himself. So when they told him the unbelievable good news, he refused to let go of his disillusionment; he didn't want to be disappointed again. He was too honest to pretend that he didn't have doubts. He wasn't going to go along with something others said just because it made him or them feel good. He was not the kind of man who would recite a creed without understanding what it was all about. And Jesus clearly respected him and his honesty, for he appeared to him specially and gave him a chance to believe.

Watching Thomas and Jesus and the other disciples, we learn a lot about doubt and belief, and about religion and faith. We learn that there's nothing wrong with a healthy skepticism and an inquiring mind, so long as we do not close off all chance of enlightenment. Thomas's magnificent profession of faith was all the stronger because, with Jesus' help, he had faced his doubts and overcome them.

We also learn that faith and religion cannot be done all alone. We need other people. Thomas was not with the other disciples when the risen Jesus first appeared to them, and that was part of his problem. In the individualistic society that is America, there are many people who try to do religion all by themselves. They say they don't need church, they can relate to God one-on-one. Jesus was willing to go one-on-one with Thomas, but even as he accepted Thomas's act of faith, he told us that it usually doesn't work that way. "Blessed are those who have not seen and have believed." Faith comes from hearing, from the words and the witness of others. The first reading, from the Acts of the Apostles, vividly describes how the early church shared and passed on the faith. "They devoted themselves to the teaching of the apostles and to the communal life, to the breaking of bread and to the prayers.... And every day the Lord added to their number those who were being saved." And that's the way we do it today: together. That's what church is all about.

The author of today's second reading praises his fellow second-generation Christians in words that are addressed to us as well: "Although you have not seen him you love him; even though you do not see him now yet believe in him,...you attain the goal of your faith, the salvation of your souls."

What part of my own story can I find in the experience of Thomas?

Third Sunday of Easter

Acts 2:14, 22–33; 1 Pet 1:17–21; Luke 24:13–35

Were not our hearts burning within us?

It was on the afternoon of the first Easter Sunday that Cleopas and his friend met the risen Jesus. There are many mysterious things about this meeting, but the first is that they didn't recognize him. There are several other instances in the Gospel accounts of the post-resurrection Jesus in which the same thing happens: People who had been close to him in life do not know him at first, but then perceive his identity in a flash of recognition.

He looked like just another friendly stranger that Sunday afternoon when he joined the two grieving disciples on the way to Emmaus. It's really Jesus, but they don't recognize him because since the resurrection his body is radically transformed. He shows an interest in them and expresses concern at their sadness and dejection. They tell him of the terrible things that have happened, the great things that might have been, the beautiful things that now can never be. It's a story of dashed expectations and of dreams laid waste. "We had hoped," they say. But we hope no longer. It's finished, and so are we.

Up to this point, Jesus was just a good listener. When people are down, the way Cleopas and his friend were, the best thing we can give them is a willing ear. If I'm scraping bottom and you're my friend, I don't want words from you. Just be with me and care.

Jesus did that and more. He speaks words not of empty comfort, but of brilliant insight. He recalls the history of their people, the story of God's ways with us. He helps them see that a suffering Messiah did not mean the end of their hopes.

After he explains to them why the messiah had to suffer and die as part of God's plan, they feel unburdened and at peace with themselves. They've reached their destination, and he starts to leave them. But it's getting dark, and the roads are not safe, so they offer him their hospitality. "Stay with us." It was a small gesture of thoughtfulness, but it reaped a great reward. In the breaking of the bread—which sounds like a Eucharist—they recognize him. He vanishes from their sight, but from now on he will always be with them; nothing can take him away.

This is how you and I meet the risen Christ—through a kind word, by an unselfish invitation, in the breaking of the Bread. He comes unexpectedly. He is not always recognized. He's glad to be asked, but he forces himself on no one. To see him, I must be as alert to the needs of others as to my own. He waits for me in the guise of a needy stranger or a suffering friend or under the appearances of bread and wine. Only the eyes of faith can pierce the veil, but one moment of vision is worth a lifetime.

Recall a time when Christ encountered you in a person or an event. Did you recognize him?

Fourth Sunday of Easter

Acts 2:14a, 36–41; 1 Pet 2:20b–25; John 10:1–10

*I came so that they might have life and
have it more abundantly.*

In today's gospel passage and in the psalm, we meet a way of talking about God that is very familiar to Christians and Jews: he is described as a shepherd, and the people as his flock. Shepherds are familiar figures in that part of the Middle East, and the imagery had a real impact on those who lived there. For us, though, pictures of shepherds and sheep don't say much. We understand the idea and have a vague notion of what shepherds do, but that's it. What is Jesus trying to tell us about his Father and himself?

A shepherd in those days led a very hard life. He was always on duty, always on the watch, patient, and fearless, to keep the sheep from wandering and to protect them from thieves and other dangers. That's the way God is: always vigilant, looking after us, protecting us from dangers that come from outside us and from within.

The shepherd's life was a dangerous one, too. Out on the open plain, there was no one to protect him from sheep-stealers; he was on his own, and sometimes had to fight to protect himself and his flock. That's why Jesus once said that "the good shepherd gives his life for his sheep" (John 10:11b). At sundown the shepherd used to gather his sheep into an enclosure that had a narrow opening; then he would go to sleep lying down across that narrow space. That's why Jesus calls himself the "gate for the sheep." Anyone would have to get past him, and maybe kill him, to get at the sheep.

Jesus was the Good Shepherd, and he laid down his life for us. Those who watch over his followers are called "pastors," a Latin word meaning "shepherd." To be a pastor in our church means always to be on call, watchful and ready to serve. Pastors have not always lived up to their calling; in recent years some have let us down badly. Some have treated the people like sheep, and some keep doing so, but that's not what Jesus had in mind. What he did have in mind, and what good pastors in our church try to live up to, is to do what Jesus did—work that their people "might have life and have it more abundantly."

Think about some good pastors you have known. Are some pastors still treating their people like sheep?

Fifth Sunday of Easter

Acts 6:1–7; 1 Pet 2:4–9; John 14:1–12

Show us the Father.

Philip speaks up for all of us when he asks Jesus, "Show us the Father." What is God like? He is so mysterious, so far beyond our grasp. Sometimes he seems so distant that we wonder if he even exists. And if he is real, do we matter to him? Does he listen to us? Does he care? Why doesn't he run a better world than this crazy, violent mess that we live in?

And Jesus answers him. "Have I been with you for so long a time and you still do not know me, Philip? Whoever has seen me has seen the Father."

We believe that Jesus came to save us; otherwise we wouldn't be here in church. But do we realize that he has come to answer the deepest questions we can put to life? He has come among us as the very revelation of God. What is God like? Jesus tells Philip and us, "The answer is right in front of you." We know an awful lot about God, because we know his son. Look at him. They bring sick people to him, and he heals them, not in crowds, but one hurting person at a time. He meets blind people and he does what you and I wish we could do: he gives them sight. His friend Lazarus has died, and he breaks down and cries. He's puzzled and hurt when people don't trust him; but when they do, he can't resist them. He gets angry when he sees people in authority acting unjustly, and he tells them off. He is brutally honest with the powerful, but tender and gentle toward the weak. This is the man we meet, Sunday after Sunday, in the Gospel. Are we listening? This is the kind of God we have! No wonder we call it good news!

Is God still mysterious? Oh yes, he is. And does he sometimes seem distant and far away? Of course he does. We're talking here about the infinite, majestic Creator of the universe. Is it surprising that we cannot grasp him, that at times he seems so elusive, even unreal? It shouldn't surprise us. But God has taken a lot of trouble to bridge the infinite gap between us and help us know him as he is. The Word was made flesh and dwelt among us. He was a baby, a child, a teenager, a young adult, a man in the prime of life who surrendered that life out of love for us. He taught us by word and even more by deed. Watch him. Listen to him. Take him at his word when he says, "If you know me, then you will also know my Father."

What are some of the words and deeds of Jesus that help me to know God better?

Sixth Sunday of Easter

Acts 8:5–8, 14–17; 1 Pet 3:15–18; John 14:15–21

If you love me, you will keep my commandments.

Jesus says that if we really love him we will keep his commandments. He doesn't make the mistake that many people make, of reducing love to a feeling, to a form of sentiment. There are children who claim to love their parents, but they disappoint them and even break their hearts because they refuse to obey the most reasonable demands. They have feelings of affection, but they don't follow through. There are husbands and wives who claim to love their spouse. They do have strong feelings of attraction and affection, but they undermine their marriage by ignoring the most basic requirements of an intimate relationship. These are forms of disobedience; they are failures to observe the requirements of real love.

When Jesus says we must keep his commandments, he's not just telling us to observe a bunch of rules and regulations. You can't reduce the Christian life, or any true religion, to a list of do's and don'ts. The Pharisees tried that, and it didn't work. They ended up with a rigid, stifling religion. But there is a place for rules: the Ten Commandments are a good start. They tell us to worship God, to respect parents, to respect life, to be sexually responsible, and to be truthful and honest. Sometimes these commandments are hard to obey; they occasionally call for courage, unselfishness, and sacrifice. These are the tests of real love.

But the Commandments are not only demanding; they are also sometimes unclear. "Thou shalt not kill" sounds simple enough, but is it? How does it apply to abortion…to war…to stem cell research…to capital punishment? These are not always easy questions. Sometimes good people can and do disagree. So Jesus doesn't leave us orphans trying to figure it out all by ourselves. He sends us the Holy Spirit to guide and help us. He calls him "the Spirit of truth, whom the world cannot accept." By "the world" he means those people who either don't believe in God or pay no attention to God. Religion plays no serious part in their lives; they simply try to impose their views on reality. Their favorite word is "choice," which they think takes care of everything. But we are not like that; we admit our need, and we look to the Spirit for guidance.

Does this guarantee that we will always do the right thing and live up to the law of love? Of course not. Life will always have its share of obscurity and uncertainty. God only asks that we do our best, that we not try to go it alone. We belong to a church that is the Body of Christ, whose vital principle is the Holy Spirit. Its leaders teach in the name of Christ and help us to discern the truth. They are human and fallible just as we are, so they and we must be attentive to the Spirit. We're all in this together, as we try to know Christ's commandments, to keep them, and thus prove our love for him.

If the Commandments are not just a bunch of rules and regulations, what are they?

Ascension

Acts 1:1–11; Eph 1:17–23; Matt 28:16–20

Go…and make disciples of all nations.

Forty days after his resurrection, did Jesus actually go up into the sky as his followers watched him leave them? Maybe. Maybe not. Maybe it was just St. Luke's way of telling us that Jesus is no longer in his earthly body, that his triumph is complete. St. Paul uses picturesque language—sitting "at [God's] right hand in the heavens, far above every principality, authority, power, and dominion"—to express his final, total glorification. What we need to know is not what the ascension looked like and how it happened, but what it all *means*.

To find out, pay attention to the angels. They bring us down to earth. "Why are you standing there looking at the sky?" Don't look up. Look around you. There's a whole world waiting to be won. Jesus made the great sacrifice and triumphed over sin and death, not for his sake but for ours. It's time to share the wealth with those who have not heard the good news. "Go, therefore, and make disciples of all nations,...teaching them to observe all that I have commanded you."

The whole world? All nations? That's a big order! Well, Jesus started small, with a few fishermen, a tax collector, some dedicated women, and a few other followers. And look at what they have accomplished. The Gospel has been preached throughout the world, down the centuries to our own day. Countless men and women have been baptized in the name of the Father, and the Son, and the Holy Spirit, enriching their lives and the lives of those around them. The surpassing greatness of his power is felt here on earth, brought to life and light in the words and deeds of those who believe in him and preach in his name.

Jesus tells his followers to make disciples and to baptize them. When it happens, we call this conversion. But that's not the whole story. Jesus does not say to just *make* disciples. He tells his followers to also *teach* these disciples all that he has commanded. This goes far beyond baptizing infants and adult converts. We are called upon not just to recruit new members but also to have an impact on the world around us. We obey his command when we work for justice, when we help the poor, when we stand up for the value of human life, when we share values that preserve and nourish what is best in people's hearts and minds. These efforts don't always attract new members to our church, but they fulfill the law of love. And that, after all, is what it means to "teach them all that he has commanded us." When we inspire others by our example to join in the struggle for human dignity and welfare, we are indeed making disciples.

So stop looking at the sky. Look around you, and see what needs to be done. The job is never over, and sometimes it seems far beyond our powers. But there's no reason to give up. Jesus himself assures us: "Behold, I am with you always, until the end of the age."

What am I doing to make disciples?

Seventh Sunday of Easter

Acts 1:12–14; 1 Pet 4:13–16; John 17:1–11a

Father, the hour has come. Give glory to your son.

On this Sunday, three days after Christ's ascension into heaven and a week before Pentecost, we see the apostles and Mary gather together to pray in the upper room where Jesus had celebrated the Last Supper. The gospel reading takes us back to the night of that supper. Jesus knows that the hour has come for him to suffer and die, and he prays to his Father: "Give glory to your son, so that your son may glorify you." How can he say that his death will bring him glory?

Jesus was one of those people, down through history, whose lives have been defined and glorified by their deaths. Abraham Lincoln was one. Joan of Arc was another. And so were Thomas More and anyone who ever died for a noble cause, and every martyr who has died for the faith. Jesus himself says: "I glorified you on earth by accomplishing the work that you gave me to do." And what was his work? "I revealed your name to those whom you gave me." But his work would not be complete until he paid the last full measure of devotion. Only by dying for us could he show us that the love of God would stop at nothing, not even at the cross. Yet the cross was not the end; the fullness of his glory was revealed in his rising from the dead.

So, in the end, death gave way to life, and not only in Jesus' resurrection and ascension. Next Sunday, on the feast of Pentecost, we will celebrate the birth of the church in the power of the Holy Spirit. St. Peter writes to us, the church, that we should rejoice when we share in the sufferings of Christ. He doesn't mean that we enjoy pain for itself, but if it comes to us because we are faithful followers of Christ, we should rejoice. Jesus himself made it clear that those who wish to follow him must be ready to carry a cross. Being a Christian and refusing to compromise with the world is going to cost us. Sooner or later it turns some people off, and they will make us pay. But Peter assures us: "If you are insulted for the name of Christ, blessed are you, for the Spirit of glory and of God rests upon you."

The disciple is not above the master. Christ's way to glory was through the cross. The same goes for us.

What is the cross that Christ wants me to carry?

Pentecost

Acts 2:1–11; 1 Cor 12:3b–7, 12–13; John 20:19–23

There are different kinds of spiritual gifts but the same Spirit.

If we are going to be honest with one another, we have to admit that we live today in a divided church. Not only are there divisions among Catholics and other Christians—Protestants, Orthodox, Evangelicals—but there are also divisions within the Catholic Church itself. Today, the feast of Pentecost, is a good time to acknowledge our differences and to think and pray about them together.

Look at the crowd on that first Pentecost. The apostles are given the gift of tongues, so that people of many different nations understand them. This reminds us of the story of the Tower of Babel, which describes the breaking up of the human race into many different languages. Pentecost represents God's power coming down and overcoming the barriers between people. Well, look at us now. On our worst days, we resemble *The Tower of Babel: Part II*.

Disagreement is not something new. When St. Paul wrote his letter to the church at Corinth, not many years after Jesus' ascension, he was addressing a community that was deeply divided over such matters as marriage, the proper celebration of the Eucharist, and the role of women in public worship. When he says, "No one can say, 'Jesus is Lord,' except by the Holy Spirit," he is reminding them that they share the life of the Spirit and should not read one another out of the church because of their disagreements. "There are different kinds of spiritual gifts but the same Spirit...different workings but the same God." No matter how serious our differences, we must never forget who we are: "In one Spirit we were all baptized into one body." We are the body of Christ.

Many Catholics find this hard to accept. How can we have different opinions and still claim to follow the same Lord? Jesus gives us a hint when he appears to the disciples on Easter Sunday evening. He tells them, "Peace be with you." That sounds like a command to be quiet and undisturbed. But then he says, "As the Father has sent me, so I send you." That's a truly inspiring thought, isn't it? Like Jesus, we are sent to be a light to the world, to enlighten, to heal, to be good shepherds, to be ready to lay down our lives for one another. But remember what it was like for Jesus. He was misunderstood and rejected. His twelve closest followers were constantly arguing among one another and jockeying for position; one of them betrayed him, and the rest deserted him. Why are we so surprised that we do not always agree on how to save the world?

Some of our disputes are not very important. They are matters of style, arising from different temperaments and personalities. We get on one another's nerves, but we can get over it. Other disputes are more serious; they bring to the surface differences we cannot and should not ignore. It is a characteristic of dysfunctional families that they cannot bring their differences to the surface and deal with them. Many noisy, quarrelsome families are actually healthier.

On this feast of Pentecost, let's not be like the apostles when they were fearful and hid behind locked doors. Let's come out in the open, speak honestly and openly to one another, confident that our sharing in the Spirit can overcome any division, pierce any darkness, heal any wound. Let us pray with confidence: "Come, Holy Spirit, fill the hearts of your faithful, and kindle in them the fire of your love."

Where do you see division in the church or in your family? How do you deal with it?

Trinity Sunday

Exod 34:4b–6, 8–9; 2 Cor 13:11–13; John 3:16–18

A merciful and gracious God, slow to anger and rich in kindness and fidelity.

Tell children about God, and they probably imagine an old man with a beard. Isn't that the first picture you had? That image inspired great art like Michelangelo's painting of the creation of Adam in the Sistine Chapel. But as we grew up, we realized that God isn't a man, isn't old, and doesn't have a beard. And the more we reflect and pray over what we have been told, the more we wonder, what is God really like?

God has meant many different things to different people in different religions and cultures. To some, God is a remote, unchanging, majestic being who rules over the world in inscrutable, undisturbed fashion. To others, God is, above all, a judge who inspires guilt and fear. Some just say that God rewards the good and punishes the wicked, and let it go at that. Then there are those who think of God as a sentimental, laid-back deity who just wants us to feel good about ourselves. And finally there is the pro-choice God who wants whatever we want.

Christians and Jews have always tried to do better than that. Within the limits of human understanding, we try to be true to a many-sided God—One who is Creator, Lord, and Judge, but also Friend, Lover, and Companion. A God who hates sin but loves sinners. A God of judgment who dispenses mercy. This is the God we meet in the readings for today's feast of the Most Holy Trinity—not a faceless, unchanging deity but a passionate, involved parent. A God whose ways are not our ways, yet who never ceases reaching out to us.

As Moses bows down to the ground in worship and asks pardon for the wickedness and sins of a stiff-necked people, the Lord passes before him and cries out, "The LORD, the LORD, a merciful and gracious God, / slow to anger and rich in kindness and fidelity." John proclaims that "God so loved the world that he gave his only Son, so that everyone who believes in him might not perish but might have eternal life." And Paul urges the Christians at Corinth: "Mend your ways, encourage one another, agree with one another, live in peace, and the God of love and peace will be with you." He closes with the prayer with which we often begin this Mass: "The grace of the Lord

Jesus Christ and the love of God and the fellowship of the Holy Spirit be with all of you." And we echo his blessing with our own song of joy: "Glory be to the Father, the Son, and the Holy Spirit; to God who is, who was, and who is to come."

How has your image of God evolved during your lifetime?

The Most Holy Body and Blood of Christ

Deut 8:2–3, 14b–16a; 1 Cor 10:16–17; John 6:51–58

Whoever eats my flesh and drinks
my blood has eternal life.

On this great feast of the Body and Blood of Christ, we are asked to remember that day, in the synagogue at Capernaum, when Jesus promised that he would give us his flesh to eat and his blood to drink. On the day before, he had fed the crowds with a few loaves of bread and some fish. It reminded them of an event that had happened a long, long time before. Almost thirteen centuries earlier, when their ancestors were on their way to the Promised Land, they ran short of food in a desert place. They unexpectedly came upon a strange new kind of food that saved them from starvation. Seeing God's hand in this saving event, they called the food manna—bread from heaven. Now Jesus had just fed them in miraculous fashion, and they all crowded into the synagogue the next day to hear him.

He spoke to them very bluntly, saying that they were at the synagogue that day because he'd given them a free meal. Food for nothing had impressed them. But he wanted to give them something much greater. He asked if they remembered when their ancestors had eaten manna in the desert. Their ancestors had been saved for a while, but eventually they died. He said to those present that he wanted to give them *living* bread. This

45

bread was his own flesh, given for the life of the world. If they ate it, they would never die. He himself would be their food and drink. His flesh and blood would be their pledge of everlasting life.

That was when prudent, sensible, and calculating people took over. They asked questions like, his flesh and his blood? *How?* And the spell was broken. Pedestrian minds took over and brought everyone down to earth. This was just too much to believe.

If all Jesus wanted to do was be popular, he should have said, which I'll paraphrase in today's language, "Well, now, hold on. Let's talk this over. Maybe you folks are taking me too literally. I didn't say you'd actually eat my flesh and drink my blood. No, I meant it as sort of a symbol. You know, like when you eat the bread and drink the wine, you'd be *reminded* of me. A kind of memorial supper, if you know what I mean." But instead of aiming for easy popularity, he spelled it out and nailed it down: "Amen, amen, I say to you, unless you eat the flesh of the Son of Man and drink his blood, you do not have life within you.... For my flesh is true food, and my blood is true drink."

This was the moment of truth. Some made the leap of faith, the act of trust, and believed him; others refused the challenge and walked away. To us who believe, Jesus says, "Just as the living Father sent me and I have life because of the Father, so also the one who feeds on me will have life because of me. This is the bread that came down from heaven…[W]hoever eats this bread will live forever."

How has my belief and participation in the Eucharist nourished me and my life of faith?

Ordinary Time

Isa 49:3, 5–6; 1 Cor 1:1–3; John 1:29–34

*Behold, the Lamb of God, who takes away
the sin of the world.*

Every time we celebrate Mass, we say, "Lamb of God, you take away the sins of the world, have mercy on us." This prayer comes from today's gospel passage, when John the Baptist points out Jesus to his followers and calls him "the Lamb of God." Where did this image come from, and what does it tell us about Jesus and his impact on our lives?

John was probably thinking of the Passover, the great saving event of the Jewish people, when God rescued them from Egypt and slavery. On the night of their deliverance, the Israelites smeared the blood of a lamb on their doorposts and were spared by the angel of death, who killed the first-born of the Egyptians. The lamb had saved them from destruction. John saw in Jesus the one who had come to save his people and take away their sins. And we know, even better than John did, how true his vision was. For Jesus went to the cross and shed his blood so that our sins might be forgiven. His victory over sin and death is celebrated in the Book of Revelation: "I looked…and heard the voices of many angels…and they cried out in a loud voice: / 'Worthy is the Lamb that was slain / to receive power and riches, wisdom and strength, / honor and glory and blessing.' / Then I heard every creature…cry out: / 'To the one who sits on the throne and to the Lamb / be blessing and honor, glory and might, / for ever and ever'" (Rev 5:11–13).

On that first Passover in Egypt, the Israelites made a sacred meal of the lamb they had slain, and then set out on their journey to the Promised Land. In a few minutes, in our own sacred meal, right after we pray to Jesus the Lamb of God, we will eat his body and drink his blood in Holy Communion. For the Lamb not only saves us from sin and death, he feeds us with himself and gives us the strength to carry on. The Bread and the Wine are food for the journey—a journey from the slavery of sin to the freedom of the sons and daughters of God.

Life is a journey. Where am I headed? How does Jesus help me find my way?

Third Sunday of the Year

Isa 8:23—9:3; 1 Cor 1:10–13, 17; Matt 4:12–23

The people who walked in darkness
have seen a great light.

Today's readings are all about *light* and *darkness*.

Isaiah says, "The people who walked in darkness / have seen a great light." Matthew sees this prophecy fulfilled in Jesus' preaching and ministry in Galilee. What is this darkness of which they speak?

We can all look back on times when we lost our way, maybe did things we are now ashamed of. We regret lost opportunities. And now we wonder, "How could I have been so blind? I was really in the dark then."

All the bad things that make the evening news and the next day's headlines make it painfully clear that there is a great darkness hovering over our world today. We live in the midst of war, terrorism, genocide, and civil strife. Into this darkness comes the Gospel, the message of Jesus Christ. At Christmas we celebrated the coming of him who is the light of the world. How could his coming pierce the darkness?

To save the world, he began by going down to the docks and signing up a few fishermen. It was a blue collar operation; he started small. And yet no one, down the ages, has had a greater impact on people's minds and hearts.

What will dispel the darkness that hangs over today's world?

It starts small...with one person refusing to hate, resolving to love

with one person refusing to be selfish, resolving to reach out

with one person refusing to despair, resolving to hope.

It starts with you and me.

Jesus calls you to be fishers of people...in your family

where you work

where you play.

Refuse to be overwhelmed by the magnitude of the task!

Maybe what we do seems so little, but remember the workers at Ground Zero. They cleared away one piece at a time. People from everywhere reached out, one at a time, to the bereaved. At the very heart of evil, goodness prevailed.

At this moment in history, we are a people who live under a cloud of uncertainty, under threat from those who hate us. But we can say with the psalmist,

The LORD is my light and my salvation; whom should I fear?

The LORD is my life's refuge, of whom should I be afraid? ...

Wait for the LORD with courage, be stouthearted, and wait for the LORD.

In what ways do I bring light into the darkness around me?

Zeph 2:3, 3:12–13; 1 Cor 1:26–31; Matt 5:1–12a

*Rejoice and be glad, for your reward
will be great in heaven.*

Today's gospel reading is the beginning of the Sermon on the Mount. At first, it sounds beautiful. On second thought, it seems all wrong. And finally, it makes a lot of sense.

The language that Jesus uses is eloquent, idealistic, inspiring. But if you listen carefully, you can see that it is directly opposed to several taken-for-granted articles of commonly accepted, so-called wisdom: The way to be happy is to own as much as you can. Pain and suffering must be avoided at all costs. Always try to be in control. Write off anyone who neglects you or doesn't appreciate you. If anyone tries to insult you, don't get mad; get even. And steer clear of the peaceniks who try to turn you into a wimpy, do-gooder, bleeding heart.

The philosopher Frederick Nietzsche found the Sermon on the Mount so offensive that he called it a prescription for sheep and slaves. But take another look at what Christ is saying and you realize, even from your own experience, how much sense he makes. Making money and owning stuff are nice but they don't guarantee contentment; conspicuous consumption can even eat you up. Pain and suffering are undesirable, but they are ultimately unavoidable; if we try too hard to avoid them, we may close ourselves off from all consolation. Being in control can be satisfying, but it is not to be sought at all costs, and it is ultimately unattainable. We will inevitably run into people who offend us and put us down; it's okay to stick up for ourselves, but at some point it's best to forgive or make up or just walk away. As for peace—well, it's not to be sought just at *any* price, but it ought to be clear to everyone, by now, that violence is even more expensive and is usually self-defeating in the long run.

So Jesus offers a program for living that turns accepted wisdom on its head. And make no mistake: he is not saying that people who live his way will have to wait until they're dead before they get their happiness in heaven. He says they are blessed right now. And in our more enlightened moments, you and I know it is so. When we look back on our own lives, we can see when we're at our best. When we're content to live simply. When we don't shrink from sacrifice. When we don't insist on being Number One. When we refuse to be poisoned by resentment. When we resist the urge to seek revenge. When we renounce violence in the pursuit of justice. If you've been trying to live this way, Jesus congratulates you and says that you are blessed indeed!

At first sight, the Beatitudes seem a long way from the "American dream." How can we close the gap?

Fifth Sunday of the Year

Isa 58:7–10; 1 Cor 2:1–5; Matt 5:13–16

You are the salt of the earth.

Jesus says that we, his followers, are called to be the salt of the earth and the light of the world. If those words mean anything at all, he is saying that by our faith we are supposed to have an impact on our world.

How do we do that? Isaiah says the most direct way is to share your bread with the hungry, to shelter the oppressed and the homeless. That's literally putting your money where your mouth is. Your faith has had an impact for good on those who need it most. You are indeed the salt of the earth.

That's simple enough; no one will argue with that. It gets more complicated when we talk about being the light of the world. Jesus says our light should shine before men and women so that they see what we stand for and may be inspired to follow our example. We're supposed to stick out like a city on a hill that no one could miss. But isn't religion a matter of privacy? As Americans, aren't we supposed to respect diversity? Most of us are not comfortable talking religion with those who do not share our beliefs. But if we try to maintain peace by keeping our beliefs and values to ourselves, how is that different from putting our lamp under a bushel? This is not an easy question.

Of course, we should respect the right of others to believe or not believe whatever they wish. In a free society, there is no place for imposing one's beliefs. That's one of the things that make us different from the Taliban. But how neutral can we be without becoming bland, like salt that has gone flat?

This became a painful issue during a recent presidential election. All of us, including bishops, struggled with the question of what we should expect of a Catholic candidate. At the heart of the controversy was the question: What is the connection between faith and action? This is a challenge not just for candidates and office holders, but also for ordinary voters like us. When you confront issues like capital punishment, national defense, tax cuts for the wealthy, gun control, and welfare, do your religious convictions factor into your decisions? Do you ask where Jesus would stand? Do you bring your religious beliefs into the voting booth, or do you leave them outside? Do you bring them into the workplace? Should you?

There's a lot of darkness all around us, in the minds and hearts of people who are confused and led astray by false values and destructive ideologies, who don't know any better. As a follower of Jesus Christ, you have something better to offer. Without being tactless or offensive, maybe you could speak up for the truth, stand up for what you believe. You might even spread a little light. Jesus would like that.

How does my faith have an impact on those around me?

Sixth Sunday of the Year

Sir 15:15–20; 1 Cor 2:6–10; Matt 5:17–37

Unless your righteousness surpasses that of the scribes and Pharisees, you will not enter the kingdom of heaven.

In this passage from the Sermon on the Mount, Jesus says that our holiness must surpass that of the scribes and Pharisees. What does he mean?

The religious leaders of his time said that murder, adultery, and lying were sins. Today we would say that that was not rocket science, it was a no-brainer. But Jesus takes it a step further. He says you don't get any prize for not actually *committing* those sins; you must not even *want* to. God cares not only about our actions; he looks deeper. In the court of heaven, we are acquitted or condemned according to what goes on in the depths of our hearts and minds.

When you think about it, it makes a lot of sense. There are many thieves who are not in jail, and not just because they haven't been caught. They haven't stolen anything, either, but not because they're honest. They're just afraid of getting caught. If they could get away with it, they would take anything that isn't nailed down. That goes for a lot of other crimes and sins, too. What looks like blamelessness may be due not to virtue but to lack of opportunity. It all started way back.

Remember when you were in the third grade and were tempted to cheat? Why didn't you? Because you were honest? Or just careful?

So Jesus says that we will be in trouble with God not just for killing our neighbor but even for being angry with her. He's not criticizing us for our emotions; we can't always help the way we feel. Sometimes we have good reason to be resentful. Repressing righteous anger solves nothing; it can even be unhealthy. He's talking about the anger that simmers and boils, the anger we nurse along from year to year. It eats away at us as we look forward to the day when we can get revenge, and rejoices when something bad happens to the person we hate. There's no law against that kind of anger down here, but it gets bad marks in heaven. And it should, because it's self-destructive.

He goes even further. He condemns not only adultery, but also lust. That's not new, either. Remember the ninth commandment? "You shall not covet your neighbor's wife." Once again, we can't help the way we feel, especially in matters sexual. But we're supposed to recognize temptation for what it is and resist it, out of conviction for what we know is right or wrong. So "coveting" is out; we're not supposed to covet our neighbor's goods, either. It's okay to *wish* we were better off, but we should try to resist envy and jealousy. We know from experience how destructive those can be, too.

This Sermon on the Mount is pretty heavy stuff. It sets the bar of goodness high, but it's worth aiming at. Just trying will make us better than we thought we could be.

How do I deal with feelings that threaten to eat me up?

Lev 19:1–2, 17–18; 1 Cor 3:16–23; Matt 5:38–48

Love your enemies and pray for those who persecute you.

People on their way to the racetrack often say, "Today I'm going to get even." Most of them don't really mean it. They say it playfully, making fun of themselves, because they know that nearly everyone who bets on horses ends up in the red. They're just looking forward to an entertaining afternoon where they might end up a few bucks ahead for a change. The only bettors who really believe in getting even are the compulsive gamblers who have a serious problem and are deluding themselves.

In today's Gospel Jesus talks about getting even. He says the old system, an eye for an eye, is like those gamblers' systems: it doesn't work. It was part of the ancient code of Hammurabi, a Babylonian lawgiver of two centuries earlier. In its own time, it was an improvement over the tribal customs that carried punishment and vengeance to extremes. But even the Jewish people before Jesus saw its limitations. In the first reading, from the book of Leviticus, God tells Moses to take no revenge and hold no grudges against his fellow countrymen. (What about foreigners? That's another story). The psalmist reminds us that the Lord is kind and merciful, slow to anger. Elsewhere in the Old Testament we read: "If your enemy be hungry, give him food to eat… Say not, 'as he did to me, so will I do to him'" (Prov 25:21; 24:29). So Jesus was not the first one to preach against vengeance. But he goes further than anyone ever has, before or since.

If we take him too literally, he sounds utterly unreasonable. Of course we have a right to legitimate self-defense. We mustn't let bullies have their way; if we do, they'll just get worse. We cannot lend money or make donations to everyone who asks us. That's not just impossible; it's irresponsible. So what is he saying?

He says that from now on, retaliation is out. Even when we have good reason to be angry, we are not to seek revenge against those who insult us or treat us unfairly. In order to be able to act this way, we have to get past the hurt feelings and renounce the kind of resentment that insists on revenge. This is a big order, and we may not feel up to it. When we're told to give up the idea of payback, we feel like the compulsive gambler who is told he must stop betting, like the addict who is told he must give up alcohol or drugs. God is showing us tough love, and it hurts. But if we don't listen, we risk hurting ourselves and others even more.

What do people accomplish when they insist on an eye for an eye? Look at the record. The Shiites and the Sunnis. The Serbs and the Croats. The Israelis and the Palestinians. And many more. Long-standing feuds and real and perceived wrongs on both sides have convinced millions that they must get even. But they never do. They only guarantee that violence will spiral out of control. Their only hope lies in reconciliation. And that goes for all of us.

How can I follow this teaching and not be a wimp?

Eighth Sunday of the Year

Isa 49:14–15; 1 Cor 4:1–5; Matt 6:24–34

Do not worry about tomorrow;
tomorrow will take care of itself.

When my father died during the Great Depression, he left my mother, a woman with a grammar school education, and three young children. She barely made ends meet. The food stamps were never enough, and she risked losing her welfare check by doing sweatshop work on the sly. When we children got to be young teenagers, we realized what was happening and became very concerned. One day we thought we were acting grown up when we went to her and told her how worried we were: what was to become of us? How could we ever get by? We thought she would be glad that we understood. Instead we were shocked when she got very angry with us. She didn't want to hear any of that kind of talk!

I was completely confused. I was too young to understand her reaction. And I never thought about it again until many years later when I heard today's readings. Isaiah says, "Can a mother forget her infant...? [God] will never forget you." Jesus says, "Do not worry about what you are to eat or drink. Your heavenly Father knows all that you need." When people hear Jesus telling them not to worry about paying the bills, they often react the way I, as a child, reacted to my mother. What do you mean, don't worry? Can't you see what's happening? There's plenty to worry about!

I understand my mother now, and I think I understand Jesus, too. She felt insulted. How could her children doubt that she would take care of them? Jesus says that we unwittingly insult God when we let worry wear us out. Don't we know that God has never let us down, and never will? God takes care of the flowers and the birds; do you think he won't watch over you? Okay, you say, but we're not flowers or birds, and we're not children. We have to work hard and be careful and save and plan ahead. Of course! He doesn't say that we should be shiftless or irresponsible. He doesn't deny that the future is often uncertain and threatening, and that we have reason to be concerned. What he is speaking against is the kind of anxiety that takes all the joy and confidence out of life and turns us into careworn, fretful prophets of doom. No Christian should be like that.

Did my mother worry? She must have. But she refused to be paralyzed by fear of the future. She cooked and mended and washed and worked and ran rings around the snoopy social worker, and she prevailed. Do you think God isn't as smart and determined as she was? He gave you and me the greatest gift of all—life. After we've done all we reasonably can to nourish that life and the lives of those we love, God is going to be there for us. That's the kind of God we have. How do we know? Jesus told us.

A wise man once gave this advice to his son who was leaving the nest and starting out: "Just do your best. The biggest troubles you have to face are the ones that never come." Reality is never quite as bad as most of our fears. That's not looking at the world through rose-colored glasses. That's looking through the eyes of Christ.

How do I combine confidence in God with reasonable concern?

Ninth Sunday of the Year

Deut 11:18, 26–28; Rom 3:21–25, 28; Matt 7:21–27

Not everyone who says to me, "Lord, Lord,"
will enter the kingdom of heaven.

There's no point in going to a doctor unless you're going to follow her advice. There's no point in consulting an expert unless you're going to use his insight. And there's no point in hearing God's word unless you're going to put it into practice.

That's what Jesus says to us who are religious and pray and go to church. We spend a lot of time saying, "Lord, Lord," but do we have anything to show for it? Actually, a great deal more than we might think. A relationship needs togetherness and communication. The quality time we spend with God, praising him, begging forgiveness, asking for what we need, and thanking him for his blessings, is the stuff of intimacy. That's why they're so important. But today he tells us to take it one step further and ask ourselves: What effect does all this have on the way we live?

We all know what Jesus is talking about when he says that some religious people live lives that contradict the beliefs they profess. Some of them are hypocrites, but most of them are not that bad; they just settle for mediocrity. They *hear* the word of God on Sunday, but they don't *listen.* It goes in one ear and out the other. They don't come to church to find out how to live. And they don't come out of church asking how they can live what they've heard.

We all fail this way sometimes. As Paul says in the second reading, all have sinned. Just think of what we hear in this church, week after week. The words of Jesus and the apostles and the prophets are sometimes inspiring, sometimes comforting, frequently surprising, and always challenging. The last few Sundays we have been listening to the Sermon on the Mount. We are told to be honest, unselfish, compassionate, and forgiving. We are to renounce lust, anger, and revenge. We're supposed to love everyone, even those who don't love us, even our enemies. This is a lot more than conventional, middle-class morality. How often do we take these words to heart and resolve to change our ways?

God says to us through Moses: "Take these words into your heart and soul. I set before you here, this day, a blessing and a curse: a blessing if you obey the commandments of the Lord, …a curse if you do not." Jesus says: "Everyone who listens to these words of mine and acts on them is 'building his house' on a rock. Anyone who listens to these words but does not act on them, is building on sand." A lot of people build their lives on sand; most of them don't know any better. But we are blessed. We have a doctor named Jesus who can heal us if we let him. He is an expert in living; all we have to do is take his advice and follow him.

Think of some ways in which faith has influenced the way I live, and some ways it hasn't.

Tenth Sunday of the Year

Hos 6:3–6; Rom 4:18–25; Matt 9:9–13

I did not come to call the righteous but sinners.

There is a paradox at the very heart of the church of Christ. We are called to be holy, yet there's a sign over the entrance: "Only sinners may apply."

We have always easily acknowledged that we are sinners. That's one of those general statements that no one finds threatening. But the scandals of recent years have shocked us deeply. It's a good sign that Catholics did not leave the church in great numbers. Most of us know better than to make hasty, unfair generalizations about priests or about the church.

Still, the scandals were widespread enough for us to draw some legitimate inferences. There has been a real failure not only of moral behavior but of moral leadership among those who should have been most trustworthy. Some long entrenched practices, like circling the clerical wagons, have been discredited. That's good. But it's only the beginning of an agonizing reappraisal that the institutional church has to go through. We're in this for the long haul.

Meanwhile, we do well to listen to today's gospel reading. The Pharisees were seriously religious laymen who were shocked at Jesus hanging out with the wrong people. The tax collectors of Jesus' time were not your basic IRS functionaries. They were part of a corrupt system imposed by foreigners on the people of an occupied nation. Men who did this work were considered traitors to their own people. Yet Jesus picks one of them, Matthew, to be in his inner circle of followers. Jesus answers the Pharisees: I came to call not saints, but sinners. Another time he says there will be scandals among his followers, but we are not to be disheartened. Neither are we to be complacent. In the first reading, God laments, O my people, what shall I do with you? Our indignation must not be like the morning dew that quickly disappears.

Perhaps the greatest temptation facing us is not self-righteousness or complacency, but discouragement and despair. Some of us feel like we've had all the hope sucked out of us. Paul, in the second reading, reminds us of Abraham, our father in faith, who hoped against hope, who trusted God's promise against all human expectation, and who was not disappointed.

Listen to Paul. Listen to Jesus. We are a church of sinners, called to be holy. We have been betrayed, but we persevere. We have been humiliated, but we hold our heads high. We have been wounded, but we will recover and maybe even emerge stronger and better in God's sight. If all we had going for us were human wisdom and determination, we would probably fail. But don't underestimate the power of God that is at work within us.

Consider some possible good effects that may be resulting from the church scandals. How do we come to terms with sinfulness and still maintain our ideals?

Exod 19:2–6a; Rom 5:6–11; Matt 9:36—10:8

*They were troubled and abandoned, like sheep
without a shepherd.*

When Jesus talks about sending out laborers to help with the harvest, he's talking about us. Not only clergy and religious men and women, but also all Christians are called to share in proclaiming the reign of God. He has an important job for you and me in sharing the Good News. But what does he mean when he tells us to "cure the sick, raise the dead, cleanse lepers, drive out demons"? How are we supposed to do *that*?

The key to understanding this mission is to understand the meaning of Jesus' miracles. They were marvelous deeds, yet meant to be more than marvels. They were *signs*, realities that pointed to something greater than themselves. But what could be greater than curing the sick and raising the dead? Well, the people Jesus healed got sick again, and those he raised from the dead eventually died again. In healing the body, Jesus was telling us that he could cure an even deadlier illness, the sickness of the spirit. And so can we.

How does Jesus send you and me to heal, to cleanse, to drive out demons, and restore to life? He tells us to make a difference to the people in our lives. What are some of the diseases that afflict people, and how can we heal them?

Sometimes they suffer from hopelessness and are close to despair; we offer encouragement and show our concern. They thought no one cared, but we do. Sometimes people close to us are slipping into mediocrity; they need us to challenge them and motivate them to aim higher. When they are tempted to give in to the demons of racism and prejudice, we may have to confront them and stand up for justice. Sometimes they just need someone to believe in them, so that they can believe in themselves.

Without realizing it, we all do a lot of this sort of thing, much of it taken for granted. Parents make sacrifices for their children and try to inspire them and give them good example. The middle-aged among us go the extra mile to care for aging parents. Friends unselfishly go out of their way to help friends. And many a generous response is given to requests to pitch in and help out those in need. Some of you have no idea how busy you keep the recording angel working overtime to keep track of your good deeds.

This is what Jesus was talking about when he told us to love our neighbor as ourselves. This is what he had in mind when he signed us up to help with his work. Let's thank God that he has given us the grace to enrich the lives of those around us. And at Communion time, when we eat the bread of life, let us draw strength to answer his call and go out and help with the harvest. God needs all the workers he can get.

Sneak a peek at the recording angel's list of your good deeds. Come on, don't be bashful. Think of someone who could use your help.

Twelfth Sunday of the Year

Jer 20:10–13; Rom 5:12–15; Matt 10:26–33

Do not be afraid; you are worth more than many sparrows.

There's a scene in Shakespeare's *Hamlet* where the young prince tells his friend Horatio, who fears for his safety, "There's a special Providence in the fall of a sparrow." He's referring to the passage in today's gospel reading. Jesus urges his followers to overcome their fear in the face of persecution...to live with integrity, no matter how great the cost. He says that even the death of a sparrow matters to his Father.

This is about more than persecution. It's about the problem of evil. Jews and Christians believe in a God who is a loving father. This God is all-knowing, all-powerful, all-just. A God who loves goodness and hates wickedness. Why, then, does God let bad things happen to those he loves?

We are not always surprised by suffering, or even by the apparent triumph of evil. What is worst is the sense of abandonment—the feeling that no one cares what happens to us, not even God. For some people, God died in the Holocaust. Christianity offers no solution to the problem of evil, but offers a response. Jesus says, "You are worth more than many sparrows." No matter what happens, we are to *trust*...to abandon ourselves to the mercy of God, confident that he will never desert us, and will give us the strength to endure and to overcome.

Time and again, in the gospels, we find that Jesus is puzzled and disappointed when the people close to him do not show him that trust. When the fishermen in the boat panic during a storm, they wake him up and ask him to save them. He says that they have little faith, then gets up and stills the storm. When Peter starts to walk toward him on the water, then loses his nerve, Jesus says to him that he too has little faith. And at Nazareth, when the people he grew up with reject him, he is amazed at their unbelief. Does he expect too much?

Think of all that God has given us, beginning with life itself...our loved ones...people and events that have shaped and enriched our lives...so many blessings we take for granted. Most of all, he has given us his Son, whose saving death and resurrection we celebrate in this Mass. When we remember all this, how can we not trust him? And even if, in our weakness, we are tempted to despair, we know that his grace is there, offering the strength we need, assuring us that he will never forsake us. In John's Gospel, at the Last Supper, he makes a promise that says it all: "In the world you will have trouble, but take courage, I have conquered the world" (John 16:33).

Have you ever felt alone and abandoned, even by God? Have you ever been disappointed by someone's lack of trust in you?

Thirteenth Sunday of the Year

2 Kgs 4:8–11, 14–16a; Rom 6:3–4, 8–11; Matt 10:37–42

Whoever does not take up his cross and follow after me is not worthy of me.

Jesus is the master of paradox, the apparent contradiction. He says, "Whoever finds his life will lose it, and whoever loses his life for my sake will find it." What does he mean?

A young father of a large family once told me that, with each new child, he felt as if he were burning his bridges behind him. He felt, more and more, the weight of his responsibilities and the realization that he did not know what lay ahead. He felt like a gambler playing for higher and higher stakes. Where did he get his nerve? From love, of course; his love for his wife and children. And here is another paradox: the less time and energy he had to spend on himself, the richer he felt. He had found himself in ways he could not have done otherwise. By being willing to lose his life, he found it.

That's the good news. The bad news, as you all know, is that more and more men are afraid to marry and to commit themselves irrevocably to wife and children. In a film several years ago, Martin Sheen played a young man who has been living with his girl friend for six months. One day she suggests marriage and is shocked at how negatively he reacts. It's as if he had touched a hot stove. He says: "You want to know what marriage is? The great sacrifice! From now on it's everything—I mean *everything*—for the kids. Your weekends are shot, working on the house. You hang on to that job you hate, because the kid needs new braces. And forget your own dreams, pal, because now it's time to send Junior to college so *he* can become Mr. Wonderful. You call that happiness?"

That's an eloquent speech, and he speaks for many. What he and they are most afraid of is losing their freedom. And freedom means "keeping your options open." For such people, choice no longer implies commitments and consequences—as making love used to carry important consequences. Choices of friends, lovers, and careers should all be subject to immediate cancellation. Such is the open-ended conception of the good life that appeals to more and more shallow people.

Well, back to the film. The lovers quarrel and the young man storms out of the apartment and goes to a bar. There he meets two jaded bachelors who are hitting on a couple of female flight attendants from out of town. He gets a glimpse of the sterile life that awaits him if he doesn't break out of his narrow, self-centered world. He returns to his girl friend and says, "Let's talk about it." The film ends, but the real story is just beginning. He's had a reality check. He now has some idea of what Jesus means when he says that those who care only for their own life will lose it. And we hope that he will discover the second part of the paradox: "Whoever loses his life for my sake will find it." Somewhere along the line the young man will discover what we all eventually learn: that it involves taking up a cross. When we take Jesus at his word and accept the cross and his offer of grace, we discover who we are and what we are meant to be. In being ready to lose our life, we find it.

Think of a way in which Jesus' paradox has been verified in your own life.

Zech 9:9–10; Rom 8:9, 11–13; Matt 11:25–30

Come to me, all you who labor and are burdened.

"My yoke is easy, and my burden light."

"Really?" Are you sure?

The last time I looked, some of the things God asks of us are not easy at all. Some of the burdens he asks us to bear are quite heavy. One or two could break your back. At times taking on Jesus' yoke can cost you money, time, convenience, and patience. Keeping the commandments often calls for real sacrifice. Keeping the Sabbath holy disrupts your schedule. Honoring one's father and mother can become very burdensome when you're middle-aged and your parents need extra special care. Not killing isn't so hard, but forgiving your enemies can make you grind your teeth. Not committing adultery is only occasionally a problem, but being sexually responsible across the board is something else again. Telling the truth is sometimes quite a challenge. And as for coveting your neighbor's goods…well, it's hard not to be jealous of those who have it better. So let's not kid ourselves; the burden isn't always light. Sorry, Jesus; no offense.

Seriously…what does Jesus mean? He knew that the way of life he was calling us to is idealistic and demanding. So why call it easy? Well, look at it this way: when someone asks you, "How's your job?" they're not just asking what you do for a living. They're asking, "What kind of people do you work for? How are the working conditions? Do you have security?"

God knows our pain, and he shares it. God went all the way and became one of us in the person of his only Son. Jesus lived in a country occupied by foreigners. He worked with his hands and lived a blue-collar life. Like us, he knew what it was sometimes to be exploited, neglected, taken for granted, misrepresented, and misunderstood. Was it hard for him? Yes and no. He was like the kid in that famous ad for Boys Town, the one who's carrying a smaller boy, who says, "He ain't heavy, he's my brother." When he carried the cross, he carried us on his back. Now he asks us to carry one another, assuring us, "Whatever you do to the least of these, you do for me."

That's the kind of God we work for, and those are the conditions. Not so bad, after all. And the security? He himself assures us: "Come to me and I will refresh you, and your souls will find rest."

Which commandment gives me the most trouble? Am I carrying anyone? Are they heavy?

Fifteenth Sunday of the Year

Isa 55:10–11; Rom 8:18–23; Matt 13:1–9

A sower went out to sow.

During my many years as a schoolteacher, I never ceased to be fascinated by the different results of my teaching. I would prepare a lesson for two or more groups of students of the same age level. In the first class, it might go rather poorly; the students were apathetic and uninterested. I would leave the room reproaching myself for not preparing a better presentation. In the next class, I would use the same outline, the same examples, the same stories, and the results were entirely different. These students responded with curiosity, interest, even enthusiasm. What made the difference? Not I, and not the lesson or the presentation; they were all the same. Obviously, it was the group. And the second class wasn't any smarter than the first; they were just more receptive. Their eyes and ears and sometimes even their hearts were open, ready for something new, wanting to learn.

When Jesus told the parable of the farmer sowing the seed, he was reflecting his own experience as a teacher. His preaching had widely different results. Forget his enemies for a moment; think of those who were not hostile. Some of these were idly curious; his message went in one ear and out the other. Some found him stimulating at first, but they were too shallow to accept his challenge and apply his words to their own lives. Others were just too busy to give him much attention. And then there were the ones whose minds were open; they recognized him for what he was—the greatest teacher of all time—and they took his lessons to heart They weren't any smarter or better educated than the others. The difference was not in their minds but in their hearts: they were open, ready for something new, something that would change their lives for the better.

We like to think that we belong to the last group. The fact that we're in church at this moment, listening to the word of God, is a good indication that maybe we do. But then we ask ourselves: just how receptive are we? How much difference does Jesus make in my life? Do I yield thirty-fold, sixty-fold, or a hundred-fold? The fact is, none of us fits exactly into just one of those four groups. There's a bit of us in all of them. God tries to speak to me in so many ways: not just in the Bible, but also in the events and the people in my life. Sometimes I hear him but I don't listen. Sometimes I'm just superficial, and God's word glides over the surface of my life. Often I'm too busy to make time to listen. And then there are the good times, when the good me shows up. I'm alert, attentive to what God is trying to tell me, ready to respond, and honest about the gap between the person I am and the one God calls me to be.

Okay, class, there goes the bell. There'll be a quiz tomorrow, and the day after that. Keep working, and we'll all do well in our final exams.

If Jesus were to give me a mark, would it be 30? 60? 100? Any way to get extra credit?

Sixteenth Sunday of the Year

Wis 12:13, 16–19; Rom 8:26–27; Matt 13:24–30

Let them grow together until harvest.

This parable of the weeds and the wheat brings to mind a famous saying of our time: "Three strikes and you're out."

During a period of great lawlessness and crime waves, some States tried to solve the problem of repeat offenders by decreeing that if a person committed three felonies, he automatically was sentenced to life in prison. This succeeded in getting some career criminals permanently off the streets; that was the good news. But after a while some bad news turned up: there were cases of petty criminals where the sentence was obviously too harsh. Judges sometimes wanted to modify the penalty, but the law was too sweeping; it denied the judges all discretion. The same thing happened in the case of drug laws. The public outcry against users and dealers was so intense that very harsh penalties were decreed—so harsh, that after a while they were seen to be unjust in their application, and efforts were made to change them.

In his parable of the weeds, Jesus says that there are good people and bad people, but that you have to be careful in trying to separate the bad from the good, or you may do harm.

The weeds and the wheat are not always easy to tell apart. It may be quite clear that some people are bad, but how bad? How dangerous? Are you sure they can't be reformed? Are you giving up on some people too soon? Jesus says, "Don't rush to judgment. Wait. Only God knows for sure, and he will be the final judge. In the meantime, beware lest in trying to do good, you do real harm."

The parable also reminds us of another famous expression: "Zero tolerance."

This wasn't about drug dealers or petty criminals. It was about priests who had betrayed their calling and done great harm to children, to young people, and to the church at large. The sheer volume of wrongdoing amounted to a moral catastrophe. Everyone agreed that strong measures were called for. The weeds had to go, period. And thus was born the formula, "zero tolerance." No more cover-ups. No more second chances. Never mind how often you did it, or how long ago, or whether you had repented and changed your ways. You were out, and you could never get back in. That made a lot of people feel better. That showed that we were serious, that we had learned our lesson.

But the question remains: Did we pull up some wheat with the weeds? How many priests, who fell briefly many years before, who repented and were no longer a danger to anyone, continued to be punished? Was "one strike you're out" the way to justice?

While you're thinking about this and praying over it, remember when Peter asked Jesus how many times he should forgive a wrongdoer. Seven times? Jesus said no—seventy times seven. Think it over.

Consider the difficulty of finding the golden mean between being too strict and too permissive.

1 Kgs 3:5, 7–12; Rom 8:28–30; Matt 13:44–46

The kingdom of heaven is like a treasure buried in a field.

If Aladdin loaned you his lamp, and you got just one wish, what would you ask for? You have ten seconds to make up your mind....

Okay, time's up. What did you ask for? Win the lottery? A free round-the-world first-class vacation? Promotion to CEO of a big business? According to some modern philosophers, whatever you picked was based on one of the three most basic human hungers—for money, or pleasure, or power. These, they say, are what make the world go 'round.

Maybe your choice fit their description, maybe not. One man who broke the mould is found in today's first reading. God tells King Solomon, "Ask something of me and I will give it to you." What does he ask for? Wisdom. "Give [me] an understanding heart,...so I can distinguish right from wrong." God's long response to his request can be boiled down to "Nice going! Good choice!"

Notice that Solomon didn't ask to be smart, but to be wise. There's a big difference. Wisdom is more than intelligence; it goes much deeper. Some of the cleverest people in the world aren't wise at all. They have the smarts, but don't know what to do with them. And many people with modest IQs have real down-to-earth wisdom.

It's this wisdom that helps us to tell right from wrong. Wisdom knows that no amount of money can buy a meaningful life. It enjoys pleasure, but keeps it in its place and subordinates it to higher goods. And it sees power not as a weapon of self-importance but as an opportunity to serve the common good. This is what Jesus calls a buried treasure, a pearl of great price, more precious than anything in the world.

Where can you get this wisdom? Some people look for it in philosophy. If that's too heavy for you, you can go to the library where whole shelves are filled with self-help books. Or you can listen to God's own word, best expressed in the person and the teachings of Jesus Christ. Here we find the clues to real self-fulfillment...what to do with money and pleasure and power... how to enjoy them without being ruled by them...where are the right places to look for happiness. This is real enlightenment, the kind that leads to action. Hear the word of God, and keep it. Listen to Jesus, watch what he does, and ask for help to do the same. And you'll be truly rich, truly wise.

In what way is my faith helping me to be wise?

Eighteenth Sunday of the Year

Isa 55:1–3; Rom 8:35, 37–39; Matt 14:13–21

All ate and were satisfied.

When we hear that Jesus cured the sick and fed the crowd, we say that he performed miracles. But the Gospel writers don't call them *miracles;* they call them *signs.* Signs point to something greater than themselves. But what is greater than curing the sick and feeding thousands with a few loaves of bread and some fish?

Psychologists speak of felt needs and unfelt needs. Two felt needs that we all have are for health and food. When we are sick, we want to be cured. When we are hungry, we want to eat. There are deeper needs, too, and we are not always aware of them.

We need to be healthy inside. We need to be honest, unselfish, responsible, caring persons...people of integrity. We need to be

73

cured of dishonesty, self-centeredness, irresponsibility, greed. These are sicknesses of the spirit. These are sin. Jesus wants to restore us to health, if we'll let him. When he cured the physically sick, he gave us a sign that he has the power to heal us at our very core.

We need food, too. Not just for our bodies but also for our spirits, so that we can be the kind of people God meant us to be. When Jesus fed the crowd, he gave them and us a sign that he would give us another kind of food. The crowd he fed that day got hungry again; but if we eat the Bread of Life, he assures us that we will never be hungry again. That bread is right here on this altar. Soon it will become the body of Christ, which we will take and eat.

There are people who seldom or never go to church; they're staying home today. Religion, for them, is not a felt need. They don't think they're missing anything, and they wonder why we feel the need. We who come to church cannot always put it into words, but we're looking for something more. We want to be healthy not only in body but also in spirit. We want to nourish that part of ourselves that seeks a fuller life, open to the infinite, open to God. In a little while we will eat and drink the body and blood of Jesus Christ. This is what the miracle of the loaves was all about.

Think of a spiritual sickness that you'd like to be cured of.

Nineteenth Sunday of the Year

1 Kgs 19:9a, 11–13a; Rom 9:1–5; Matt 14:22–33

O you of little faith, why did you doubt?

The first President Bush, as a young man, had served in the parachute corps. So, on his eightieth birthday, he celebrated by jumping out of an airplane. He forgot to pull the ripcord, but fortunately the men with him took care of it and he landed safely. Some people would say that, at his age, he should have known better than to try. But you have to admit that the old boy had a lot of nerve.

I don't know about you, but I say that trying to walk on water takes even more nerve. In the middle of a fierce storm at 3 a.m., the men see Jesus coming toward them and think it's a ghost. He calls out to them and says they shouldn't be afraid; it's really he. Peter says that if it's really him, to say to join him across the water. Jesus tells him to come. And Peter does! For the next few moments, Peter was able to do something he never would have imagined. What made him so brave? Faith! He believed in Jesus and trusted him.

So what happened? He took his eyes off Jesus and looked at the wind and the waves, and he began to sink. Jesus grabbed him and dragged him with him into the boat. Does Jesus say that it was a nice try or that next time Peter should be more careful? No, he says, "O you of little faith, why did you doubt?"

We all run into big storms in our lives. Sometimes the wind gets so strong and the waves so high that we feel like we're sinking. Just trying to go on seems as pointless as trying to walk on water. Sometimes what gets us through the storm is refusing to give up on ourselves. Sometimes it's the faith that others have in us. And sometimes it's faith in God. As long as Peter kept his eyes on Jesus, he was all right; when he looked away and focused on the wind and the waves, he was lost. It's the same with us. If we see only the obstacles, we lose heart. If we focus on what we have going for us, we have a chance, and we can go on.

Peter was a brave, impetuous man. He was a risk-taker, and Jesus liked him for that. He was disappointed that Peter's faith faltered, that he didn't trust him all the way. Time and again, in the gospel narratives, we notice this about Jesus. He always responds to faith; when curing people, he tells them it was their faith that healed them. And he seems surprised when he runs into lack of faith. When the people from his hometown couldn't believe in him, he couldn't do anything for them. He wants to do a lot for you and me, and he will, if we let him. Don't look at the waves. Look at him.

What are the storms that Christ can help me face?

Twentieth Sunday of the Year

Isa 56:1, 6–7; Rom 11:13–15, 29–32; Matt 15:21–28

I was sent only to the lost sheep of the house of Israel.

Today's gospel story is about crossing boundaries.

Jesus has crossed the border of his own country and is staying briefly among non-Jewish foreigners. He has not come there to teach or heal; he is determined to work only among his own people. So when the Canaanite woman asks him to cure her daughter, he shows us a side of himself that is unfamiliar and disturbing. He seems cold and remote. He ignores her and turns a deaf ear to her pleas. She gets noisy and keeps after him. The whole scene is so embarrassing that the disciples tell him get rid of her. So what does he do? He insults her. That would have discouraged most people, but not her. She is deadly earnest in her persistence; she'll take insults, but she won't take no for an answer; she's fighting for her child's life. And she wins!

What's going on here? We know that Jesus was God, and we think of him as clear-eyed, determined, and unshakeable. And he usually was, but not this time. It's obvious from this passage that the Canaanite woman made him change his mind. In a real sense, she converted him. We are reminded here of the truth of what we say in the Creed, that he was not only true God but also true man. Like us, he had to work things out and be willing to change. This is just one of several times in the gospels where we see him moved by the power of prayer. Once again he finds the faith and trust of others irresistible, and he cries, "O woman, great is your faith!"

In curing the child of a Gentile, Jesus crossed a boundary of his own making. He was a Jew, a member of God's chosen people. For centuries Jews thought this meant that God had rejected all others, but by his lifetime many of them had gradually come to see that God wanted them to be a light to the Gentiles as well. After Jesus left the earth, the early church had a hard time deciding that the faith was to be preached to all nations. It took us many more centuries to realize that even those who have not heard the gospel could be saved. And in recent years our best thinkers have pondered whether and how God reveals himself to those outside the faith.

Crossing borders is exciting, but it can also be frightening. Think of the boundaries that have been crossed in our own lifetime. We have come a long way, in a short time, from the days of racial segregation and discrimination. The rights of women and their place in society have expanded dramatically. Our attitudes toward homosexuals have undergone a sea change in the last few years. These changes have not been welcomed by all; they have provoked their own divisions, and we're still working on the implications. We know that change is not always for the better, and we have to pick our way carefully. But the sense of progress is unmistakable. Maybe Jesus felt that way, too, when he healed his first Gentile, a little Canaanite girl.

Are there boundaries I may be thinking of crossing, where faith may show me the way?

Isa 22:19–23; Rom 11:33–36; Matt 16:13–20

Who do you say that I am?

Shortly before his last journey to Jerusalem, where suffering and death await him, Jesus gathers his closest followers around him and asks: "Who do people say that I am?" Then: "Who do *you* say that I am?" And today Jesus asks us: "Who do *you* say that I am?" (My emphasis both times.) We must, each of us, answer for ourselves.

Peter's answer was, "You are the Christ, the Son of the living God." As members of his church, you and I acknowledge Jesus as the Christ. Today, and every weekend, during the Creed, we say, "We believe in Jesus Christ, true God and true man." Jesus tells Peter that he knows this only through a revelation from God, and the same goes for us. Only by God's grace do we know him. As St. Paul writes, "No one can say, 'Jesus is Lord,' except by the Holy Spirit" (1 Cor 12:3).

Peter's act of faith was the beginning of the church. It is in the church, the body of the faithful, that we come to Christ. In this church, the leaders are the successors of the apostles. They teach and govern and try to show the way to God. Jesus gives them the keys of the kingdom of heaven, and he gives them and us the guidance of the Spirit. This is how we come to Christ: with others, the members of his body.

God calls each of us by name; and, like Peter, we must answer the question, "Who do you say that I am?" But we are never alone in our faith; we are always with others. The church is made up of people—limited, imperfect people like you and me. It's too messy for some people who try to go it alone. We Americans are a very individualistic people. Some have called us a nation of lone rangers, even when we do religion. There is a young woman, a nurse named Sheila, who has actually named her religion after herself. She told an interviewer: "I believe in God. I'm not a religious fanatic. I can't remember the last time I went to church. My faith has carried me a long way. It's Sheilaism. Just my own little voice."

Well, we wish her all the best. But that's not our way. This is where we find God, here in this church, among these people. Here we listen to his word; here he gives himself to us in amazing intimacy, in Holy Communion. From here we go forth, strengthened by the Bread of Life, to try to live as if we believe what we say: that Jesus is the messiah, the son of the living God.

Does the church help me find God, or does it get in the way, or both? How?

Twenty-Second Sunday of the Year

Jer 20:7–9; Rom 12:1–2; Matt 16:21–27

Get behind me, Satan!

If you can remember as far back as last week, you may recall that in the gospel reading just before this one, Jesus named Peter the leader of the apostles and the head of his church. Today he calls Peter a devil and tells him to get out of his way. What's going on here?

Well, once Peter and the others acknowledge him as the messiah, Jesus decides it is time to tell them where all this is leading: that he must go to Jerusalem and suffer and die and rise again. That is a shock, and Peter exclaims that they would never let that happen to him. He speaks as a friend, out of loving concern…and he gets called a devil. He doesn't know it, but in telling Jesus to avoid the pain and suffering, he is tempting him to turn aside from his destiny. Now Jesus knows that he must put all his cards on the table and clear this up once and for all. He turns to the disciples and tells them and us what is involved in following him. It means carrying a cross. From time to time, somewhere along the line, we may have to give up our security, rearrange our priorities, sacrifice comfort, and say no to self-indulgence. If we're afraid of losing these things and hold on to them, we risk losing our very selves. "Whoever wishes to save his life will lose it."

So the secret is out. Being a Christian isn't easy. Following Christ is going to cost. At that moment Peter must have felt like the prophet Jeremiah, who complains to God that he'd been duped, and that he had no idea what was involved in being a prophet. And if we accept the challenge and treat our religion not as a hobby but as a way of life, we will have some of Jeremiah's experience. He says, "I am an object of laughter; / everyone mocks me." Think of the society in which we live. People are too polite to laugh at us out loud, but they think we're pretty strange. Look at the stuff we do: we make vows and try to keep them, we stand up for life across the board, we advocate sexual responsibility, we engage in strange rituals of worship, and we seek fulfillment in ways that go beyond conspicuous consumption. They can't believe we're serious! That's why Paul advises us: "Do not conform yourselves to this age but be transformed by the renewal of your mind."

Okay, so the price is high. But is it right? Maybe you noticed something that Peter missed. Jesus said he must suffer and be killed and on the third day be raised. When Peter heard about suffering and dying, he stopped listening and missed the part about the resurrection. You and I have an advantage over him; we know how the story ended, in Jesus rising from the dead. The cross looked like utter defeat, but it was the ultimate triumph. That's what it was for Jesus, and that's what it is for us.

We already know, from experience, the truth of Jesus' saying: "Whoever loses his life for my sake will find it." And full payment will come when the Son of Man comes with his angels in his Father's glory.

At what times, in my experience, has religion had to go beyond a hobby to a way of life?

Twenty-Third Sunday of the Year

Ezek 33:7–9; Rom 13:8–10; Matt 18:15–20

Whatever you bind on earth shall be bound in heaven.

"If you see something, say something." That's what the signs say on buses and trains and in stations. Be vigilant. Speak up. You could stop something bad from happening.

That's also what today's readings say. The prophet Ezekiel says you must warn the wicked person to turn aside from sin. St. Paul says that loving your neighbor means not stealing or murdering or committing adultery. Jesus says that if your brother has sinned, speak to him alone or with others. All three men, speaking in the name of God, are telling us that if we see people sinning, we are supposed to tell them to stop. But that could make you very unpopular. People may tell you: "Mind your own business." "Respect the right to privacy." "Don't impose your morality on others." "Don't pass judgment; it's unAmerican."

But Jesus doesn't back down. He says, if the wrongdoer won't listen to you, tell the church. And so today the church speaks out on a variety of issues. Adultery. Abortion. Euthanasia. Assisted suicide. Cloning. Sperm banks. War. Capital punishment. Extramarital sex. Some people wonder: Should the church be making pronouncements on these difficult issues?

81

Shouldn't we just mind our own business and leave people alone to do whatever they think is right? Isn't that the American way? It depends. Is the law of love being violated? Are people getting hurt? Are anyone's dignity or rights being violated? God, through Ezekiel, says, "If...you do not speak out to dissuade the wicked from his way...I will hold you responsible."

Think about some times in the past, in this country, when injustice was not confronted. The church was slow to speak out against slavery. We were late arrivals in the struggle against racial segregation and discrimination. When American citizens of Japanese descent were interned on the Pacific coast after Pearl Harbor, no one said anything. And during the long, frustrating struggle to obtain for women the right to vote, the church was silent. If we refuse to learn from history, we are doomed to repeat it.

This is not about putting people down or interfering in people's lives or passing judgment on them. It's all about obeying the law of love. As daughters and sons of the one God, we are family, and we have to look out for one another. That means that when people are harmed or put in danger, we must speak up on their behalf. As Ezekiel says, we must warn the wicked to turn aside from their sin. It may make us unpopular with some people because we make them uncomfortable. But that's all right. When people are doing harm to themselves or others, the last thing they need is to be comfortable or complacent. Love sometimes requires that we tell it like it is. If you see something, say something. That's what Jesus did, and he expects us to do the same.

Have there been times when perhaps I should have spoken up or acted differently?

82

Sir 27:30—28:9; Rom 14:7–9; Matt 18:21–35

Not seven times but seventy-seven times.

When Peter asked Jesus how often he should forgive someone who wronged him—seven times?—he probably expected Jesus to say, that seven times were too many. People would walk all over Peter. As a matter of fact, two highly respected rabbis of his time taught that three times were the limit. Instead Jesus says *seventy-seven times*. In other words, there must be no limit on your readiness to forgive. That's a big order! It goes deeply against the grain, especially when we have suffered wounds that are slow to heal.

How can God expect this of us? Well, for a moment, think not about what the other person has done, but about what your anger is doing to you. The beginning of the first reading is eloquent: "Wrath and anger are hateful things, / yet the sinner hugs them tight." If you've ever nursed a grudge for a long time, you know how resentment can eat you up. In wishing we could hurt others, we do damage to ourselves.

We're not just talking about feelings here. If I have been treated badly, I may good reason to feel resentful, and I don't have to apologize for it. But I must try to get beyond the offense, and reject the temptation to take revenge. If I don't feel up to forgiving, then I must pray for the grace to do so. God doesn't ask the impossible; he only asks us to do our best with his help.

Jesus backs up his advice to Peter and to us by telling a disturbing parable. The meaning is clear. If we refuse to forgive, then we cannot be forgiven. And how much forgiveness do we need? The unforgiving servant—that's us—has just been forgiven a huge debt by the king—that's God. And then he turns around and refuses to forgive someone who owes him a paltry sum of money. His outrageous behavior clearly marks him out as the bad guy in this story. If that makes me uncomfortable...well, that's why Jesus told the parable: to make me uncomfortable.

One last point. At the end of the parable, the king sentences the offender to torture until he pays his debt. What about "seventy-seven times"? Doesn't God follow his own rule? Yes, but only if we let him. The unforgiving debtor has closed off all chance of redemption. He has locked himself up and has sealed himself off from the very experience of pardon. That's scary. But it doesn't have to be this way. The psalmist says, "The Lord is kind and merciful, slow to anger, and rich in compassion." With his help, we can be the same.

Have there been times when my anger has done damage to me?

Twenty-Fifth Sunday of the Year

Isa 55:6–9; Phil 1:20c–24, 27a; Matt 20:1–16a

Are you envious because I am generous?

You have to be pretty old to remember this one. Back in the 1930s, parents used to celebrate George Washington's birthday by giving their children toy hatchets, in memory of the legend about young George chopping down the cherry tree. When I was about seven or eight years old, my mother made an error that was unusual for her. She gave my brother, who was four years older, a wooden hatchet; I got a cardboard one. Big mistake!! I didn't say anything, but my nose was out of joint for days. How could I enjoy my hatchet, when my brother had a better one?

The parable in today's Gospel is about men who didn't work the same hours but got the same wages. And *they* weren't happy, either. The lesson is not about just wages; it's about God's generosity. He asks the complaining workers, "Are you envious because I am generous?"

Sometimes we get so hung up on making comparisons that we don't allow ourselves to enjoy God's gifts. Cardboard hatchets come in many models; what's yours? Is it being less talented than someone else? Is it being less wealthy, less fortunate than others? Is it being less healthy or less handsome or less beautiful than someone else? Is it driving a Chevy while someone else has a Cadillac? What's ironical is that so many people envy *us*. They'd give anything to have our cardboard hatchets.

If St. Paul ever had this problem, he had gotten over it by the time he wrote to the Philippians. He says he's willing to accept a short life or a long life, whatever God wants. He took to heart what the psalmist said: "The Lord is good to all, just in all his ways, and holy in all his works."

Some of you enjoy the popular TV show, *Everybody Loves Raymond*. One of the characters is Robert, a forty-year-old who is still resentful because he's convinced that his parents have favored his younger brother. Most of the time he is lovably funny, but also kind of sad; he should have gotten over it long ago. Sibling rivalry is all right for children. But we adults, who are all children of God, should be beyond that. Let's rejoice and be thankful for what we have. Let's be happy for others even if they have more than we, and be glad that God loves us all. We should not be envious because God is generous. In a family of grownups, there is no place for envy.

Are some of my hatchets made of cardboard? How can I enjoy them?

Ezek 18:25–28; Phil 2:1–11; Matt 21:28–32

Which of the two did his father's will?

We all know people who talk a good game but don't perform. The chief priests and elders whom Jesus was addressing were like that. They were deep into religion, serious about ritual, regular in worship, and careful in their observance of religious rules and regulations. But outside the temple they didn't live up to the ideals and values of their faith. The beliefs they professed didn't have much impact on the way they treated their neighbors. It was all talk and no action. They were living contradictions, disappointing to God, and Jesus had to tell them off.

There's another group of people whom we also know. They don't get involved in religion. They hardly ever pray, except maybe in moments of desperation. They rarely show up in church. Yet there's a lot of good in their lives. Jesus offers two examples: tax collectors who worked for a corrupt, oppressive system, and prostitutes. He says that when you add up the lives of some of these social outcasts, they measure up, in God's sight, better than those of some religious leaders. We ourselves know of many people who are not social outcasts; they're just not formally religious. Yet they seem to live up to the ideals of our religion better than many of those who profess it.

These undeniable facts lead people to draw some wrong conclusions. Some say that religion is hypocrisy, since people don't live up to it. Others decide that religion is unnecessary, since many good people do quite well without it. How are we to answer them?

The key lies in understanding the parable of the two sons. Jesus is not praising either of them; they are both very imperfect people. Neither son is the kind that brings joy to a father. The one who obeyed in the end is better, but he comes across as surly and disrespectful. He does a good thing, but he spoils it by the way he does it. As for the corrupt tax collectors and the prostitutes—well, they're not going to make the all-star team, either. Until they clean up their act, God cannot be happy with them. He just won't give up on them. For that matter, he doesn't give up on the priests and elders, either. Jesus says the outcasts will enter the kingdom *before* them, not *instead of* them.

The ideal son is one who obeys his father and does so with graciousness and respect. The ideal son or daughter of God is one who serves God gladly...who praises him, thanks him for his blessings, spends quality time with him, listens attentively to his word, and then puts it into action. That's real religion—not just words, not just deeds, but words *and* deeds. That's going first class to the kingdom of heaven.

How do we deal with family members who no longer practice the faith?

Twenty-Seventh Sunday of the Year

Isa 5:1–7; Phil 4:6–9; Matt 21:33–43

The kingdom of God will be taken away from you.

The people who write novels and songs and make movies and television series often tell stories of unrequited love. It's a theme that touches the hearts and minds of people rich and poor, humble and famous. It sometimes gives birth to great art and tragic figures like Shakespeare's Othello, who "loved not wisely, but too well."

The Bible, which tells of God's dealings with the human race, is that kind of story. Over and over again we see God reaching out to his people, enveloping them in his love, and then being disappointed by their failure to respond. Today's readings touch on the high and low points of this ill-starred love affair. Speaking through Isaiah, God asks, "What more could I have done for you?" The psalmist recalls how God delivered the Israelites from bondage in Egypt, and wonders how they could have drifted so far from the Lord. Jesus tells the story again to a hostile audience and points out his own role in the tragedy. He reminds the religious leaders of their people's history: how God sent prophets to call them back, and those prophets were rejected and even killed. And what does God do—write them off as a bad investment? No, he sends his own Son! Here indeed is a God who loved not wisely but too well, for in one final outrage, they killed his Son, hanging him on a cross.

Jesus concludes the parable with a warning to his enemies that there will be a terrible day of reckoning. "The kingdom of God will be taken away from you and given to a people that will produce its fruit." We must be very careful in the way we take this saying. We may be tempted to conclude, "Oh, that's why the temple and the Jewish nation were destroyed. They were punished for rejecting Jesus Christ." That kind of misreading has contributed to anti-Semitism down the centuries. A second mistake is to be complacent and see us Christians as their deserving replacements. The Jews are still God's chosen people. And we indeed have also been chosen, but that means we have a lot to live up to.

We have no reason to feel complacent or superior, but we have plenty of reason to be grateful. Isaiah couldn't imagine what more God could do for us, but he didn't know that God would send his own Son. We do. We know we have been loved far more deeply than we could ever imagine or deserve. How have we responded? As a church, we have sometimes yielded a rich harvest, but it is also painfully clear that we have fallen far short of what we should be. We are trying to heed Jesus' warning and pick up the pieces. And as individuals, we must each try to live in such a way that God's love affair with us may have a happy ending.

Think about what goes into a good relationship, and then ask: How's my love affair with God coming along?

Twenty-Eighth Sunday of the Year

Isa 25:6–10a; Phil 4:12–14, 19–20; Matt 22:1–14

Many are invited, but few are chosen.

If you go to a wedding, you'll probably have a good time. Weddings are happy occasions. Even the in-laws who aren't so sure of one another usually enjoy themselves. Everyone knows that this day is the start of something beautiful and wonderful; we wonder how it will turn out for the bride and groom, and we wish them the best.

When you think of your Christian faith, does it seem like an invitation to a happy celebration? For many people, when they think of religion, that's the last thing that comes to mind. Those outside our faith often feel sorry for us. They see us as limited by all kinds of rules, weighed down by all those commandments, all those "thou-shalts" and all those "thou-shalt-nots." From the outside, it can look pretty grim.

Even on the inside, within our faith, some of our fellow Christians are afraid to enjoy life. They're so serious about being saved that they're afraid to lighten up and laugh a bit on the way to heaven. At various times in history and in various places, such activities as card-playing, dancing, and drinking and gambling in moderation have been forbidden. On Sundays in some places, even sports have been a no-no; playing is "baaad." And there have been serious theologians, who should have known better, who wondered out loud if Jesus in his lifetime ever laughed, and speculated that he probably didn't. When I was a young priest, I was advised not to try to tell any jokes from the pulpit, because even if they were funny, people would be afraid to laugh. And you know what? They had a point.

How did this killjoy spirit creep under our tent? It's not hard to figure out. The world is full of people who go to excess in trying to gratify and enjoy themselves. They misuse good things and harmless things and do a lot of damage to themselves and others. They drink too much. They bet over their heads and blow the rent money. They enjoy sex in irresponsible ways. In trying to do something about these very real problems, religious people sometimes overreact and try to throw out the baby with the bath. If other people make too much of a good thing, they will make a rule against it. And so churches become associated with long faces and blue noses. It's not what Jesus had in mind. He himself was accused of being a drunkard and hanging out with the wrong people, but he didn't let that stop him. And as long as we enjoy, in moderation, the good things that God has given us, neither should we.

Isaiah had figured it out a long time ago. He wrote: "The LORD of hosts / will provide for all peoples / a feast of rich food and choice wines, / juicy, rich food and pure, choice wines…. / [He] will wipe away / the tears from every face…. / Let us rejoice and be glad!"

Think of ways in which our church encourages us to have a good time. How do I take advantage of them?

Isa 45:1, 4–6; 1 Thess 1:1–5b; Matt 22:15–21

Repay to Caesar what belongs to Caesar.

The enemies of Jesus laid a very clever trap for him. If he said people should not pay the taxes imposed by the Roman government, he could be reported to the police. If he said they should pay the taxes, he would incur the anger of his fellow citizens who deeply resented having to pay unjust tribute to an occupying power. It looked like a no-win situation until Jesus went right to the heart of the matter: "Repay to Caesar what belongs to Caesar and to God what belongs to God." In their battles with Jesus, his enemies were on a losing streak, and this was just one more defeat.

So Jesus won the argument. But he leaves us with questions. What does belong to Caesar, and what belongs to God, and how can you tell the difference? He doesn't say. At first sight, it may look as if he has cleverly dodged the question without really giving the answer, but not if we look more closely. Jesus' way was not to make rules, but to state principles. That's why his teachings endure and speak to every age: rules change as situations change, but principles are forever. And the principle he lays down here is as basic as the first commandment: "I, the LORD, am your God....You shall not have other gods besides me" (Exod 20:2, 3).

When Jesus says we should give Caesar what is coming to him, he tells us what everyone knows. Citizens owe loyalty and obedience to their country. The government provides the safety and services that make life livable, and has the right to demand that everyone contribute to the common welfare. In the realm of law, the nation is the highest authority. But in the realm of morality, it is not. In matters of conscience, the power of the state is not absolute. Anyone who does not see this is unconsciously guilty of idolatry. When we salute the flag, we pledge allegiance to one nation *under* God, not the other way around.

Well-meaning people have often been confused about this. Every so often, especially in times of war, we hear the slogan, "My country, right or wrong." During one of our recent wars, an American officer was prosecuted and convicted of war crimes when he supervised the systematic murder of hundreds of unarmed civilians, mostly women and children. In his defense, he claimed to be following orders, and said, "I'll put the will of America above my conscience always. I'm an American citizen."

Most of us will never have to make such life-or-death decisions. We are fortunate to live in a country where citizens are not routinely faced with such stark choices. And it is not always clear when the choice has to be made. People can have honest disagreements and follow different drummers. Jesus did not make rules, but his principle stands. If, God forbid, we ever have to choose between God and country, God comes first.

The last few wars have caused deep divisions in our country. How do I deal with a conflict of loyalties?

Thirtieth Sunday of the Year

Exod 22:20–26; 1 Thess 1:5c–10; Matt 22:34–40

The whole law and the prophets depend on these two commandments.

When Jesus was asked which was the greatest commandment, he answered by giving not one but two: Love God, and love your neighbor. The two go together; you can't have one without the other. But that's not obvious to everyone. You've

92

heard of the person who said, "I love God alright; it's people I can't stand." On the other hand, there are those who do love people, whom they see, but wonder how they can be asked to love God, whom they do not see. So Jesus' answer to the lawyer raises some good questions. What are we to make of this poor, overworked word called "love"?

First of all, we know that love is more than a feeling. It is often accompanied by warm feelings, but it goes much deeper. Those we love most deeply are sometimes exasperating and disappointing; our love for them resides not in our emotions but in our hearts. Love is a matter of the will and of the mind; it gives strength and makes demands; it calls for sacrifice. Jesus himself once said that there is no greater love than this: to lay down one's life for a friend. St. Paul describes love this way: "Love is patient; love is kind; love is not envious or boastful or arrogant or rude....It bears all things, believes all things, hopes all things, endures all things" (Cor 13:4–5, 7; NRSV). That's a big order, but we do live up to it sometimes, or at least come close, when we're at our best.

How can we tell if we're obeying this commandment to love our neighbor? The rest of the Ten Commandments spell it out. Honor your parents and take care of them when they need you. Do no harm. Be honest and truthful. Don't steal. Be sexually responsible. Don't be envious or greedy. Sometimes we need help to figure out what these commandments imply. "Thou shalt not kill." Does that include abortion...war...stem cell research...capital punishment? Some of these questions are harder than others; in trying to work them out, we must ask ourselves what love demands, and the teaching church is supposed to help.

This command to love the neighbor is intimately bound up with the command to love God. The ultimate reason why people are precious is because they are made in the image and likeness of God. And herein lies the answer to that other question: How can I love God, whom I do not see? Think about the finest qualities of the most admirable and lovable people you know. Do you know why they are so wonderful? Because they are made in God's image. The whole creation mirrors the glory of God, but nothing more so than a human person. And if God still seems vague and elusive sometimes, remember what Jesus told Philip at the Last Supper. Philip asked Jesus to show them the Father. And Jesus asked in return how they could have been with him for so long and still not understand. When someone sees Jesus, they see the Father. Look at Jesus. That's what God is like. What more do we need?

Am I able to love people I dislike?

Thirty-First Sunday of the Year

Mal 1:14b—2:2b, 8–10; 1 Thess 2:7b–9, 13; Matt 23:1–12

Observe all things whatsoever they tell you,
but do not follow their example.

In today's gospel, Jesus deals with a problem that is, unfortunately, very familiar to us. He is addressing a crisis of religious leadership. The Scribes and the Pharisees have let the people down. Instead of giving inspiration and good example, some of them have done a great deal of harm and others have just settled for mediocrity. In the face of these outrages, what were the people to do? Jesus gives very good advice that applies both to them and to us.

The first thing he does is to remind the people of the God-given authority that the leaders possess. "The scribes and the Pharisees have taken their seat on the chair of Moses." That means we owe them obedience. "Do what they tell you, but do not follow their example." The sex scandals involving the behav-

94

ior of priests and the irresponsibility of bishops has caused people to wonder whether they want, any longer, to be part of this church and to profess this faith. Jesus' answer is quite clear: we are a church of sinners from top to bottom. He warned us that there would be scandals. So we are right to be shocked but maybe not so surprised; and we are not to lose heart. The message of the kingdom stands, no matter how corrupt the messenger. "Do what they tell you, but do not follow their example."

If this is a hard saying, consider this command: "Call no one on earth your father; you have but one Father in heaven." He is not talking about titles of respect given to members of the clergy; that's not important. He is telling us something much more important: not to confuse religious leaders with God himself. Only God is all-wise, all-holy, all-perfect. His word comes to us through men who are not always wise, sometimes far from holy, and never perfect. If that isn't a recipe for disaster, it certainly opens the door to the possibility of scandal. When we expect too much from fallible human beings, we make ourselves vulnerable to disillusionment and cynicism.

The only solution is for us to conduct ourselves like mature, adult believers. Give religious leaders respect, but not worship. "Call no one on earth your father; you have but one Father in heaven." There is no place in our church for the cult of person. The more we put our fellow human beings on a pedestal, the greater the damage to all of us when they fall.

This does not mean that we should accept wrongdoing by those in high places, in a spirit of resignation. Being adult means not being passive. So the next step is the sharing of responsibility by all, both clerical and lay. That is the next great task that confronts the church.

How do I deal with the disillusionment brought on by clerical irresponsibility and failed leadership?

Wis 6:12–16; 1 Thess 4:13–18; Matt 25:1–13

You know neither the day nor the hour.

We will always be tortured by two questions about 9/11: Why did we not see it coming? Why were we not prepared? And today, years later, the same questions confront us: When are the next attacks coming? And, Are we prepared?

In today's gospel reading, the parable of the wise and foolish virgins is about being ready, being watchful, being prepared. It had a special meaning for the ones who heard it from Jesus' lips. They were the Jews, the chosen people. Their whole history should have prepared them for the coming of the Son of God, but the men and women of Jesus' time were not ready; they were caught unprepared. And what is the parable's meaning for us, here and now? What are we supposed to be ready for? Death? But there is no predicting the end of our lives; Jesus reminds us that we know neither the day nor the hour. The same goes for terrorist attacks. We can try to predict them, but with no assurance. What we can do is be ready…by the way we live this day, this hour, this minute.

The foolish virgins learned, too late, what we have all learned at some time in our lives: that some things cannot be put off until the last minute. We found that out when we were in school and put off studying for a big exam. As adults, we may live with regrets for having missed opportunities because we waited too long to get ready. Hurricane Katrina caused death and destruction when those responsible failed to prepare. The foolish virgins also learned, too late, that some things cannot be borrowed at the last minute. You cannot borrow a relationship with God. Just being around religious people isn't enough;

you have to work at it and possess it yourself. You cannot borrow character, either. Just associating with industrious and responsible people is no guarantee that integrity will rub off on you and make you an honest man or woman. You yourself have to try to do the right thing, day after day.

The best advice is to imitate the wise virgins. Did you notice that, when the bridegroom showed up, they were asleep? But it was okay, because they had oil in reserve. We don't have to live in constant fear and anxiety—not about terrorist attacks, and not about the state of our souls at the hour of our death. We just have to do what needs to be done in order to be prepared; that's *all* we can do. The rest is in the hands of God.

Look back on a time when I was caught unprepared. Am I putting off something important?

Thirty-Third Sunday of the Year

Prov 31:10–13, 19–20, 30–31; 1 Tim 5:1–6;
Matt 25:14–30

Well done, my good and faithful servant.

"You gotta be in it to win it!" That's what the people say who run the Lotto, in order to get you to play. You can agree or disagree that it's worth the gamble, but you can't argue with the basic premise: that in order to win any game, you have to play, and that means taking a risk of losing. Nothing happens on the sidelines.

The man in the parable who buried his money stayed on the sidelines. He figured he would break even, but Jesus says he actually ended up losing. Whom is he talking about?

When Jesus told this story, he was aiming it at the scribes and Pharisees. They were men who took religion seriously, but they reduced it to a mountainous collection of rules and regulations and insisted that nothing could ever be changed. They turned God into a stern bookkeeper who presided over a religion that was becoming rigid and lifeless. Jesus stood for something new and exciting, so they became his enemies. This sort of thing happens to all organized religions from time to time. The guardians of the faith try to protect it from change. Not all change is good, but living things must obey the law of change or they die. Try too hard to protect the church from change, and you risk turning it into a museum whose riches must be carefully preserved. The church is not a museum; it's a living thing that must grow and flourish and meet the challenges of a changing world.

The parable of the talents is not just about religion. God gives talents not only to churches but also to individual men and women, and he expects a return on his investment. When we talk about being "gifted" we usually apply it to people of extraordinary talent. But God gives every one of us some gift, some talent, some quality that can enrich the world around us. Some have been given much, and some have been given little, but no one is left out. Some of the most anonymous, apparently insignificant people are making headlines in heaven. Maybe it's the love and care we give our family; maybe it's the energy and optimism we bring to work; maybe it's the interest we take in others and the affirmation and encouragement we spread around. In these humble ways we make the most of what we have been given, to contribute to the common good.

One last word about talents. As you know, they have to be kept active. If you're a good golfer, you must practice. The same is true if you're a musician, or a writer, or an artist, or a cook. If you stop trying to get better, you'll lose what you have. Keep trying to be a better Christian. Don't bury your talent. It's the rule of life: You gotta be in it to win it.

What is my gift? How do I use it to contribute to the world? Are there times I have "buried" it instead of using it?

Christ the King

Ezek 34:11–12, 15–17; 1 Cor 15:20–26, 28; Matt 25:31–46

When did we see you hungry?

Thinking of Christ as king is somewhat difficult for Americans and others who live under democratic governments. Monarchy is a rather dated institution; even where it endures, it is mostly ceremonial. Because absolute rule can easily degenerate into tyranny, we prefer a separation of powers among the legislative, executive, and judicial branches of government. But down through history there have been many examples of good kings who ruled wisely and well. They promoted the welfare of their people, respected the dignity and the rights of all their subjects, and enacted and enforced just laws. They rewarded the good and punished the wicked and earned the love and respect of those they ruled. Some of them were even recognized as saints.

This is what the church had in mind when it instituted the feast of Christ the King. There are several ways in which Jesus fits the description. In his time on earth he went about doing good, using his power to heal; today, in his church, he offers forgiveness and reconciliation. He stood up for the poor against the greedy and defended the weak against those who oppressed them, and his church is committed to carrying on that work. He fed the hungry with loaves and fish, and now, in the Eucharist, he offers us himself as the Bread of Life.

There is a theme that shows up from time to time in the literature about royalty. In the story, the king goes out among his people, disguised as a simple peasant, to see what life is like for the poor and the lowly. He is treated by others roughly or without respect by people who would never dare to behave like that if they knew who he was. And later, when he reveals his identity to them, they are mortified. "If only we had known that it was you!" And, like all rulers good and bad, the king has the last word.

In today's gospel, in his description of the last judgment, Jesus Christ the King has the last word. He will come in all his power and glory to reward the good and punish the wicked. Then we will be judged by how we obeyed his law, the law of love. If we fed the hungry, clothed the naked, and sheltered the homeless, he will say to us: "Come, you who are blessed by my Father. Inherit the kingdom prepared for you from the foundation of the world.... Whatever you did for one of the least brothers of mine, you did for me."

Christ the King moves among us today in disguise. Where do you see him?

Solemnities That Displace Sunday Readings

Presentation of the Lord Feb. 2

Mal 3:1–4; Heb 2:14–18; Luke 2:22–40

You may let your servant go / in peace,...for my eyes have seen your salvation.

Forty days after Jesus was born, Joseph and Mary brought him to the Temple in keeping with the Jewish law of purification. A first-born male child was always consecrated to the Lord in a special way. They remembered the first Passover in Egypt, when the angel of death slew the first-born of the Egyptians but spared the children of the Hebrews. From that day forward, a child was seen as a special gift of God, and the parents made a symbolic offering to redeem their child. The offering made by Mary and Joseph was the one offered by poor people. Jesus was going to grow up in modest circumstances, in a home of working people, like most of us.

His parents were amazed at what Simeon and Anna said about their son. Here were two people who were very much alive and coping quite well with the challenges of old age. Unlike some senior citizens, they had not yielded to the temptation to grow bitter and narrow and to live in the past, or to live exclusively for mindless social activities, forgetting who and what should really be important in their lives. They were looking forward to a better time in the future, trusting in God to bring it about, and now they see in this child the future fulfillment of their hopes and dreams. This revelation came to them in the Temple, where they spent much of their time seeking union with God in prayer and worship.

Simeon is so overjoyed at seeing the newborn messiah that he says his life is complete, and God may call him at his pleasure. But first he prophesies about the child. Jesus is destined for the fall and rise of many in Israel. He will be opposed and rejected by many, and they will bring great grief to those who love him. No mother wants to outlive her children, but Mary's heart will be pierced by a sword. Jesus will be a man about whom no one can be neutral. Either we are with him, or we are against him. This is no good old plastic Jesus, offering consolation on the cheap; this is a man who calls to decision. If we stand with him, we will be among those who Simeon said were destined to rise. And with him, we can say, "My eyes have seen your salvation,…a light for the revelation to the Gentiles, / and glory for your people Israel."

What things in my life indicate that I stand with Jesus, not against him?

Birth of John the Baptist June 24

Isa 49:1–6; Acts 13:22–26; Luke 1:57–66, 80

What…will this child be?

Today we celebrate the birth of John the Baptist, the man who first called attention to Jesus and who paved the way for his saving ministry. The birth of John caused great rejoicing in his neighborhood, because his parents were advanced in years and had just about given up hope of ever having children. Another reason for the celebration was the fact that the baby was a boy. In that society in those days, when a woman was ready to give birth, the friends and neighbors would gather at the house and would bring musicians with them. If the announcement came that the child was a boy, the musicians would strike up the band and join in the celebration, and a party would break out. If it was a girl, there was a big letdown, and the musicians packed up their instruments and went home. Those were the *really* bad old days. Anyway, there was much rejoicing, because Elizabeth finally had a child and it was a son.

Not only the birth of John but also his naming caused a great deal of comment. As in most societies, Jewish children in those days were usually given names that were familiar among the parents' families. The name 'John' was not such a name, but that was what the angel had told his father Zachary to give him; this had come especially from God. Another custom in those times was to give a name that expressed the parents' hopes and expectations for their son or daughter, and 'John' was very appropriate. It is a shorter form of a name that, in Hebrew, means "gift of God," and it expressed Zachary and Elizabeth's unexpected joy. And when Zachary approved the name and recovered his speech, it was one more event that caused a sensation.

Family and friends always wonder what is in store for a newborn child: what will his or her life be like? The unusual circumstances surrounding John's birth caused even more comment and speculation. We today, centuries later, know what a great destiny was in store for John. He was to prepare the way for Jesus. We read in the prophecy of Isaiah,

> The LORD called me from birth,
>   from my mother's womb he gave me my name....
> He made me a polished arrow,
>   in his quiver he hid me....

I will make you a light to the nations,
   that my salvation may reach to the ends of the earth.

Today we celebrate the birth of this great servant of God, and we sing, "You, child, will be called prophet of the Most High, for you will go before the Lord to prepare his ways" (Luke 1:76).

What plans do I think God had for me when I was born?

Ss. Peter and Paul June 29

Acts 12:1–11; 2 Tim 4:6–8, 17–18; Matt 16:13–19

Upon this rock I will build my church.

Today is the feast of Saints Peter and Paul. The church was founded by Peter and spread by Paul. Jesus commissioned Peter and assured the church of his protection. Jesus stood by Paul and gave him strength to bring the Gospel to the wider world.

Peter was a man who suffered from a bad case of overconfidence and three times denied Christ. Paul was a reformed bigot who used to harass and persecute Christians. These were the men that Jesus chose. They weren't perfect, they had real weaknesses, and at first they were found wanting. But they were passionate men of conviction, totally committed to what they believed in. Simon was so loyal that Jesus gave him a new name: Peter, which meant rock. Once Paul realized that it was Jesus whom he was persecuting in his followers, he was started on a mission that turned that church into a worldwide movement to spread the Good News of salvation.

Peter and Paul had made mistakes, but they repented and were forgiven. They became steadfast under persecution and finally gave up their lives. Their commitment to Christ and the church made them heroes who have inspired countless men and women down the centuries to follow them in the service of God.

It is obvious from today's headlines that Jesus still chooses imperfect people who need forgiving. But he stands by them, as he stood by Peter and Paul, and he stands by us. And he stands by his promise to Peter: that the gates of hell shall not prevail—not then, and not now.

What does Christ see in me, that he chooses me to help spread the Gospel?

Transfiguration of the Lord Aug. 6

Dan 7: 9–10, 13–14; 2 Pet 1: 16–19; Matt 17:1–9

This is my Son, my beloved, with whom
I am well pleased.

When we read this account of the way Jesus was transfigured on the mountain, we find it mysterious and fascinating, but we are not amazed. Since we believe in Jesus as the Son of God and the Word made flesh, we are not surprised that for a few moments his divinity shone through. But it was different for Peter, James, and John. True, they had seen him do wondrous things. They had watched him heal the sick and raise the dead and quiet the storm. They could see that he had been given great power by God. But they could not think of him as God himself. He was so human. He could get tired and hungry and excited and disappointed and sad, just like they did. It would be a long time before they came to the realization of what we say so easily every Sunday—"God from God, Light from Light, true God from true God, begotten, not made, one in Being with the Father. Through him all things were made."

105

The mystical experience on the mountain was a hint, a beginning of that great revelation. When the cloud descended upon them, they were reminded of those solemn events in their people's history. Moses met God in a cloud on the mountain. God came to the Tabernacle in a cloud. A cloud filled the Temple that Solomon built. The Jewish people had come to associate a cloud with God's coming. Years later, when he had put it all together, Peter wrote: "We had been eyewitnesses of his majesty. For he received honor and glory from God the Father when that unique declaration came to him from the majestic glory, 'This is my Son, my beloved, with whom I am well pleased.' We ourselves heard this voice come from heaven while we were with him on the holy mountain." Gradually the early Christians came to recognize that it was Jesus of whom Daniel wrote that he "received dominion, glory, and kingship...His dominion is an everlasting dominion / that shall not be taken away, his / kingship shall not be destroyed."

None of this was clear to the disciples that evening on the mountain. They were baffled and confused. A few days earlier, Jesus had told them that he was going to Jerusalem to suffer and die. These same three men would be present at the Agony in the Garden and would see Jesus at his lowest point. And on Good Friday, all would seem lost. Only on Easter, after Jesus rose from the dead, did they begin to understand what they had seen on the mountain. They now realized that in the midst of suffering and rejection and death, when all their hopes were dashed and they felt abandoned by God, God himself had been with them. And Thomas, speaking for them all, would exclaim, "My Lord and my God" (John 20:28).

We have all known days when we have felt lost and abandoned, even by God. Today's feast helps us pierce the veil of confusion and disappointment and to see that God is always close to us. It helped the disciples to keep going through the hard times, and it can do the same for us.

How does the thought of Jesus' victory over death help you in your dark moments?

Exaltation of the Holy Cross Sept. 14

Num 21:4b–9; Phil 2:6–11; John 3:13–17

So must the Son of Man be lifted up.

A controversial movie came out a few years ago, produced by Mel Gibson, depicting the death of Jesus Christ by crucifixion. All the critics, both for and against the film, agreed that the portrayal of Christ's torture and death was accurate and realistic…so much so, that many found it too painful to watch. For people who in ancient times witnessed actual crucifixions, the cross was a horrible symbol of suffering, shame, and degradation. If you visit the catacombs in Rome, you will see painted on the walls near the tombs of Christians not a crucifix but a fish, which was a code word used in the underground church during persecutions. If you wanted to convert people to your faith, a cross was the worst way to attract them.

Today's feast is the exaltation—the lifting up—of the holy cross. The expression "lifting up" is used in two senses in the New Testament. Sometimes it means that he was lifted up on the cross. Sometimes it means he was lifted up to glory at his ascension. The one could not have happened without the other. For Jesus, the cross was the way to glory; if he had avoided it, if he had taken steps to escape it, as he might easily have done, there would have been no glory for him. It is the same for us. If we like, we can choose the easy way and refuse the cross that each Christian is called to bear. But if we do, we

107

lose the glory. Serious athletes have a down-to-earth way of putting it: "no pain, no gain." There is no Easter Sunday without a Good Friday—not for him, and not for us.

Today's readings tell us something not only about the cross and Jesus and us, but also about God. John says, "God so loved the world that he gave his only Son, so that he who believes in him might not perish but might have eternal life." That's the Gospel in a nutshell. And it clears up a common misconception about God. Some people think of God as being stern, angry, and unforgiving, and of Jesus as being gentle, loving, and forgiving. It sounds as if Jesus did something that changed God's attitude toward us, from condemnation to forgiveness. But this text tells us that it was with God that it all started. It was God who sent his Son, and he sent him because he loves us. He even sent him to die for us, to show us the way to eternal life. And so we celebrate the lifting up of the cross of Jesus Christ, to inspire us to carry our own cross and be raised with him to glory.

What is my cross, and how am I carrying it?

All Souls Day Nov. 2

Wis 3:1–9; 1 Cor 15:51–57; John 11:17–27

I am the resurrection and the life.

Some of us are old enough to remember when the priest wore black vestments on this day. They were also worn during funeral Masses and Masses in memory of the dead. Nobody questioned it. Black seemed like a good color to express sorrow at the death of our loved ones.

I grew up in an Italian-American family, and my own impression of wakes was that they were very sad occasions. As a young adult, I was surprised to hear from my Irish-American friends that their wakes were usually cheerful affairs, lubricated by drinks and indulging in happy stories of the late dear departed.

After the Second Vatican Council in the 1960s, the Irish approach came into vogue in the universal church. The black vestments were put in mothballs, and now the priest wears white, a color that, at least in this culture, seems more cheerful. The church remembered what today's readings tell us. They are all about hope. In the face of death, which seems to mock all our aspirations, we are assured that death does not have the last word. By his cross and resurrection, Jesus has won for us a life that nothing can take away.

The point of the gospel story is really not the resurrection of Lazarus. He had been brought back to life, but he would die again. The raising of Lazarus is a sign pointing to something more important—that Jesus himself is the resurrection and the life. It is the kind of life that we celebrate in white vestments at Easter, when Jesus breaks through suffering and death and emerges into the fullness of life. It is the kind of life we celebrate today, when we profess our belief that the souls of the just are in the hand of God, that they have left us only for a while, and that we are destined to be reunited with them.

We Christians are a hoping people. Because we believe the Good News of Jesus Christ's victory over sin and death, we reject all cynicism and despair. At Mass we pray, "Dying you destroyed our death, rising you restored our life; Lord Jesus, come in glory." We believe Jesus when he says, "I am the living bread that came down from heaven; whoever eats this bread will live forever" (John 6:51). With Saint Paul we proclaim, "Death is swallowed up in victory. / Where, O death, is your victory? / Where, O death, is your sting? / …Thanks be to God who gives us the victory through our Lord Jesus Christ."

Are there some departed close to me, who bring me joy and comfort when I recall how they lived their lives?

Ezek 47:1–2, 8–9, 12; 1 Cor 3:9c–11, 16–17;
John 2:13–22

[Jesus] was speaking about the temple of his body.

Today we celebrate the dedication of the Basilica of St. John Lateran, the oldest church in Rome and, in a special way, the pope's church. We usually think of St. Peter's that way, but the pope is bishop of the diocese of Rome, and St. John's is his cathedral church, so we pay it honor every year.

A church is a place where we go to meet God. We know God is everywhere, but in church we feel his presence in a special way, in prayer and worship and sacrament. We also know that the church is not just a sacred building. It is *us*—you and I, all of us. Paul tells us in the second reading, "You are the temple of God, and the Spirit of God dwells in you." This is the same Spirit that raised Jesus from the dead, the Spirit that has come to renew the face of the earth. In the first reading Ezekiel describes the temple as a source of life; we have the power to be a source of life for all those we meet. We often exercise that power without even thinking about it. By being persons of faith, by living lives marked by honesty, generosity, integrity, and compassion, we enrich the lives of those around us. We give hope and good example to those who struggle.

These are comforting and inspiring thoughts, but there is also a shadow side to today's picture of the church. In the gospel reading, Jesus finds that the temple, his Father's house, has been turned into a marketplace. We know that that wasn't the last time the church was defiled. We are a church of sinners; from time to time the church has been soiled by greed and mismanagement and injustice. The last few years, we have become painfully aware of our sinfulness.

Over and over again, we have to repent and change our ways and try to live up to our calling. It will always be that way. But we should never lose heart. Jesus tells his enemies, "Destroy this temple and in three days I will raise it up." Down through the ages, enemies have tried to destroy the church. In our own time, we have come face to face with self-destructive forces within the church itself. We struggle with troubling issues: shortage of priests, closing of parishes, the rights of women, and the voice of the laity in church governance. But Jesus stands by his promise: he will raise us up. He always has; the ancient and venerable church of St. John Lateran in Rome has stood for centuries as living testimony to that. So are all Catholic churches throughout the world that celebrate this feast today. And so, in a small but very real way, are we.

What are the forces and the people in the church that give me hope in these difficult times?